FABULOUS
FROCKS

FABULOUS FROCKS

Jane Eastoe & Sarah Gristwood

PAVILION

CONTENTS

Introduction   8

Chapter One:
    Changes 1908–1958   12
Chapter Two:
    Changes 1959–2008   32
Chapter Three:
    Must Have   52
Chapter Four:
    Classical   74
Chapter Five:
    Fantasy   96
Chapter Six:
    Sex   118
Chapter Seven:
    Feminine   142
Chapter Eight:
    Art   164

Timeline   187
Index   192
Bibliography   196
Acknowledgements   197

Previous page: Jacques Fath's evening dress of striped silk organdie, c.1954. Fath, 'the couturier's couturier', was famous for his luxuriant, feminine evening dresses. For a brief period in the early fifties, before his untimely death, his name was often spoken in the same breath as that of Christian Dior.

Left: Supermodel Linda Evangelista wears a 1992 Valentino ready-to-wear evening dress. The dramatic (and photogenic) combination of black and white has been a celebrity favourite since the beginning of the century.

This page: Taffeta shantung dresses from the fifties – the epitome of structured femininity. 'In 1958 we looked alike in full-skirted calf-length dresses, long kid gloves and tiny hats...Whether the dress had been made by a couturier...or run up by the deb's mother's village dressmaker, the final effect was curiously similar.' *Last Curtsy: The End of the Debutantes*, Fiona MacCarthy.

Introduction

There is something about a dress. No other garment carries such a weight of fantasy: the first party dress, the little black dress, the wedding dress...As Simone de Beauvoir famously said: 'One is not born a woman, one becomes one.' And nothing helps you become a woman more than a dress. The dress is a look to die for, to save for, one that deserves time, thought and speculation – it makes a statement not only about who you are, but who you want to be. Dresses capture the mood of a moment and have the Zeitgeist woven into their very fabric: Audrey Hepburn in *Breakfast at Tiffany's*; Princess Diana on the steps of St Paul's; Twiggy waiflike in a mini; Chanel in one of her own revolutionary frocks.

We divide our dresses into eight themed sections. Sexy or feminine, classically pure or clad in colourful fantasy; we can all wear each and every one on the right day. As Hollywood's great costume designer Edith Head once said: 'Clothes have to do with happiness, with poise, with how you feel. You never forget the dress or suit in which you looked well, felt right, and lived wonderful moments – the "Alice Blue Gown".'

The selection in this book is a purely personal choice. Everyone has their own favourites. The more so since the last century has seen drastic changes of style – hemlines swing from ankle to thigh, outlines alternate between body-hugging and bell-shaped – but the fascination of the dress, this most iconic of garments, has not gone away.

In examining dresses from the past 100 years we were struck by how frequently and unexpectedly themes and styles recur down the decades. It was Coco Chanel who said that 'Only those with no memory insist on their originality', and fashion itself has not hesitated to acknowledge that the revolutionary is often grounded in history. British designer Bruce Oldfield describes fashion as 'a gentle progression of revisited ideas'; and Christian Lacroix agrees. 'The forward-looking/backward-looking nature of fashion is indisputable'.

The sharp cut of a Roland Mouret dress from the noughties echoes a Dior dress of half a century before; a 1950 shot of two models relaxing in Claire McCardell outfits is so far ahead of its time, it looks like a moment in modern day New York. The sideways glimpses of bare flesh in Versace's famous 'safety pin dress' had already been seen in the seventies, when Norman Parkinson photographed Givenchy on Jerry Hall, and the crystal chunks on Dolce and Gabbana's recent evening dress recall the shards of mirror that bestrew a 1920s gown.

Looking through these pages, we hope you will agree that nothing can lift your spirits like a really lovely dress. We all dream of, as Jean Rhys put it, 'the perfect Dress, beautiful, beautifying, possible to be worn.' In *Flowers for Mrs Harris*, Paul Gallico created a cleaning woman whose dream was for once in her life to step out of her drab existence and buy a Dior frock:

> Mrs Harris had attained her Paradise. She was in a state of dreamed-for and longed-for bliss. All of the hardships, the sacrifices, the economies and hungers and doings-without she had undergone faded into insignificance. Buying a Paris dress was surely the most wonderful thing that could happen to a woman.

> ## *"A Paris dress makes one feel capable of charming a pearl out of an oyster."*
> ### Dior model Jean Dawney

Previous page: Buyers at a Dior fashion show are shown the inverted flower design of this evening dress. The photograph was taken in spring 1947, the season in which Dior launched his legendary 'Corolle' collection, better known as the New Look. 'I created flower women', Dior said, 'with tiny waists like stems and skirts belling out like petals.'

Left: A head-turning, hot-pink silk balloon dress, encrusted with shimmering multicoloured drops by John Galliano for Christian Dior, 2008.

chapter ONE

Changes
1908–1958

It is, said Christian Dior, not just a designer but an age that makes a dress, and certainly the great revolution in fashion of the early twentieth century came out of the changes in society. The innovations of the designer Paul Poiret between 1904, when he opened his own salon, and 1914 have been hailed as 'the start of modern fashion' in that the concept upon which they were based, that of the natural figure, has been integral to fashion ever since. Indeed, it has been claimed that the freedom to abandon the whalebone or steel corset in favour of the elastic girdle 'did more to liberate women than the vote'. For of course, Poiret – whose ideas gained wide publicity with a book of his designs published in 1908 – was working at the time of the suffragettes, as well as of art nouveau and the vogue for the Orient, of Diaghilev's Ballets Russes, with their exotic and colourful costumes and sets designed by the artist Léon Bakst. As Lady Diana Cooper remembered (using a phrase that would come to epitomise a later fashion revolution): 'There was a general new look in everything in those last years before the war – a Poiret-Bakst blazon and a budding freedom of behaviour that was breaking out in the long last end of Victorianism.'

Working on the foundations laid down by Jeanne Paquin, the 'Mother of Modern Dress' (and perhaps influenced by the recent developments of 'reform' and 'aesthetic' dress elsewhere in Europe), Poiret introduced the Empire line. He was showing what were effectively the high-waisted, slim-skirted dresses of a hundred years earlier, to be worn without corsets, and made not in the lacy pastels of the belle époque but in the bright colours of the Fauve painters: 'Reds, greens, violets, royal blues...I took each tone at its most vivid, and

I restored to health all the exhausted nuances,' Poiret said. But Poiret's emancipation of women only went so far. This was also the man who in 1910 introduced the hobble skirt, which, if not broken up by hidden slits or pleats, could constrain a woman's movement as effectively as any of the elaborate Edwardian confections could do.

The First World War brought a change. The hobble skirt was impractical for women working in factories, and the new necessities saw the arrival of A-line dresses with their hems several inches off the ground, and sensible styles such as the coat frock. After the war was over, Poiret seemed *démodé* – a fashion like his lampshade tunic of 1912, its circular skirt wired out over an underdress, only worked for a class who had never felt the need to concern themselves with practicality. The pre-war couturiers would fight against the incoming '*garçonne*', or 'flapper', look. But as one reporter put it: '*Le couturier propose, la femme dispose.*' All the same, without Poiret's rejection of the corset none of the next developments would have been possible, from the drapes of Madeleine Vionnet to the supple simplicity of Chanel.

Previous page: '*Les Cerises*' – an empire-line '*toilette de campagne*' by Paul Poiret,1913, after an illustration by Georges Lepape in the *Gazette du Bon Ton*. The years before the First World War saw the flowering of Poiret's revolutionary, corset-free styles.

Right: Crêpe, tie-front dress by Jeanne Paquin, the 'Mother of Modern Dress', c.1928, showing the short-skirted, waistless fashion that characterised the late twenties.

If one name is associated with the changes of the 1920s, it has to be that of Coco Chanel. Decades later, Mary Quant would say that 'Coco Chanel invented modern clothes.' As Chanel herself put it: 'The First War made me.' Perhaps the predominance of female designers (Lanvin, Vionnet, Grès, Schiaparelli) in 1920s Paris was itself something of a revolution, but Chanel in particular reflected the new spirit of freedom and activity. 'I make clothes women can live in, breathe in, feel comfortable in and look young in,' she said. In the first half of the decade she introduced sports suits and cardigan jackets, and chemise dresses made out of cotton knit; soon came the little black dress, hailed by *Vogue* in 1927 as 'the new uniform of the modern woman'.

So ubiquitous has it become in the decades since that it is hard to imagine now just how startling was the idea of putting fashionable women into a colour and a plain fabric traditionally worn only by widows and maidservants – how startling the idea that true elegance might lie in a garment so simple (and so capable of carrying a busy woman right through from day to night) that anyone might wear it. Through all the changes in fashion since – from the cocktail frocks of the 1950s to the collections of the reborn House of Chanel today – the powerful pull of the little black dress has never gone away.

Left: Evening gowns by Lucien Lelong, 1935. Hemlines dropped again after 1930, and both the clinging line, and the back décolletage, were typical of the ensuing decade. Even the style of the photograph – two models in dresses of contrasting colours – was a recurrent motif.

Chanel had started out, appropriately enough, adapting men's clothing for women's wear. And ironically, she was in some ways an anti-fashion designer – one whose strong personal style of clothing would reappear almost unchanged after World War II, and can still be worn today. It was Chanel who said prophetically that: 'A happy find is only there to be lost again.' In the mid-1920s the waistline dropped and the hemline rose; bright young things bound their breasts. But the famous flapper heyday was shorter than one might think.

The end of the twenties saw the Wall Street Crash and the start of the Great Depression and, as so often, the crisis in confidence seemed to call for a return to a more conventional femininity. There is a story from this moment in the history of twentieth-century dress that proves 'revolutions' in costume really can come overnight. The designer Jean Patou had stood alongside Chanel in the drop-waisted, short-skirted urge to modernise but suddenly, in the autumn of 1929, came a moment when he realised he was now seeing more of his female clients' legs than an officer and a gentleman of his generation ever expected to see. He rushed from the studio, tore up the existing drawings for the next collection and replaced them with – oh, the shock of it! – a waistline in its natural place and a dropped hem. Overcome with trepidation, he stood behind the scenes as the collection was unveiled, until his assistant brought the news: '*Ça marche!*' In the first row women were trying to tug their skirts down over their knees. 'Patou bomb drops – skirts reach ankles,' *Vogue* wrote. It was one of those moments when everything from the day before becomes instantly old-fashioned: in Hollywood several films (their costumes now quite laughable) were left languishing in the can.

What followed was a kind of Indian summer return to luxury in dress, as well as to styles which hugged the figure. The thrusting Hollywood film industry played its part, ensuring that ever more lavish costumes could be seen – and aspired to – by women who lived and moved far from high society. But all too soon the coming of World War II called a halt to the frivolities – and, it would turn out, to one city's dominance of the fashion industry. Americans had been among the most lavish buyers at the Paris collections of spring 1940, but after France fell the famous couture houses were closed to them, and the fashionable had to look elsewhere for inspiration.

In Europe war slowed everything down. Dresses had to last; shapes had to be slim and sparing of fabric; and garments had to do from day through evening – the 'war-wise dress' was how *Vogue* described it. While women in England struggled with draconian clothing restrictions and the rigours of the skimpy 'utility frock', America's response to the new mood took some more interesting forms. The simple lines and relaxed fit of the dresses designed by Claire McCardell – a basic tube of material bound at the waist, or a print dress loosely tied at the side – made them ideal for the burgeoning ready-to-wear market, without relinquishing the style and drama associated with more exclusive dress.

The memory of McCardell's clothes may still be evoked today, when a magazine runs a fashion spread on bright shift dresses or even 'city shorts'. But they are far from the pre-eminent fashion image we recall from the 1940s. It took Paris a year or two after Liberation to reassert the dominance of its imagination, but in 1947 Christian Dior – announcing that it was his dream 'to save women from nature' – presented the 'Corolle' collection, better known now as the 'New Look'.

Nothing is ever wholly 'new'. The seeds of revolution can take a long time to germinate. The intensely feminine look Dior defined and popularised, with its longer skirts and nipped-in waists, harked back to the belle époque – but more interestingly, it had briefly been seen in many of the haute couture collections of 1939, including those of Mainbocher, Rochas, Lelong and Molyneux. Back then, before war put an end to the reckless consumption of fabric, *Vogue* had said that a woman's only essential was 'a tiny waist, held in if necessary by super-light-weight boned and laced corsets'. Balenciaga had already started working along the same lines as soon as war ended, in 1945; across the Atlantic, Claire McCardell too had decided the time was right for an admittedly far simpler and less structured line of full-skirted dresses falling well below the knee. As Dior himself put it: 'It happened that my own inclinations coincided with the tendency of the times.' But after the austere lines of the European war years, the impact of the flower-like, demanding 'New Look' was indeed extraordinary. There was – at a moment when women were being urged into a return to femininity and domesticity – something enchanting in the very impracticality of skirts so wide they could hardly be accommodated in even the largest limousine.

Left: Wartime shot of a model wearing a neat checked dress from 1943. The dress is made of spun rayon, the popular fabric of the war years, and patriotically posed in front of a recruiting poster of Uncle Sam.

> *"Claire [McCardell] could take five dollars' worth of common cotton calico and turn out a dress that a smart woman could wear anywhere."* Norman Norell

As *Vogue's* fashion editor wrote from America: 'I was conscious of an electric tension I had never before felt in couture...We were witnesses to a revolution in fashion.' In France, Françoise Giroud, editor of *Elle*, declared that: 'Yesterday unknown, Christian Dior became famous overnight.' But Carmel Snow, the legendary editor of *Harper's Bazaar*, had the lasting word: 'It's quite a revolution, dear Christian. Your dresses have such a new look.'

Dior's designs were greeted with a gale of criticism. In a Britain still hard-pressed by rationing, official sources protested against the sinful waste of fabric. Newspapers buzzed with the angry comments of women who had tasted the freedom of the working world and feared the constrained femininity of the new clothing. It was claimed that this brave New Look had developed in the Paris of Occupation, and might be linked to fascism; that the expensive impracticality of the new style heralded an unwelcome return to elitism; that it was out of tune not only with the mood of Britain,

but with the direction in which American fashion had moved. But in the US, the consumers who made the boom of post-war America (and the magazine editors who guided it) proved to have appetite enough to swallow even fifteen yards of fabric to make a day dress. The complainants could not win – and, having discovered his power, Dior kept up the pressure. Over the next decade he rang the changes on the female silhouette with almost every collection, from the swirling 'Corolle' shapes to 'Spindle' designs that, while they still depended on emphasising the female form, did so by clinging tight to the body. Even in the fashion-conscious fifties, however – the 'golden age of couture', the age of the designer as dictator – there were movements afoot that would presage the next great revolution.

The youth revolution of the 1960s had its birth in the 1950s and before. As far back as 1938 Claire McCardell had made extensive use of a simplified shape, tied at the waist with a sash or belt to fit the wearer, with her groundbreaking 'Monastic' dress. In 1954, Chanel (the former champion of women's sartorial liberation)

Right: The 'American style', of which Claire McCardell was a leading pioneer, made extensive use of homely fabrics such as gingham, as seen in this dress of 1947.

came out of retirement to raise her standard all over again, in protest at the 'idiocies' she saw all around her. 'A dress must function or *on ne tient pas*. Elegance in clothes means being able to move freely.' But ironically it was Cristobal Balenciaga, that artist of the elite haute couture, the 'master of us all', as Dior called him, whose dramatic experiments with form and length, with statement and simplicity, did most to prefigure the coming changes.

Balenciaga – who, wrote Cecil Beaton, 'uses fabrics like a sculptor working in marble' – created straight tunics and billowing balloons, or backs and collars that stood out from the body. Balenciaga (like Chanel, like Vionnet, of whom more in the 'Classical' chapter, *see pages 74–95*) disliked change for its own sake, and after the war said that 'No sweeping changes should be made until this period of transition has settled.' But it would be Balenciaga, often described as a prophet, who first showed high boots and mini-culottes on his catwalks; and

it was Balenciaga who, along with his protégé Givenchy, throughout the fifties developed different versions of the sack and the simple tunic shape. In 1957 both men showed chemise dresses; as too did even Christian Dior. In 1958, following Dior's untimely death, the young Yves Saint Laurent, who had become the new director of the House of Dior, was hailed for his introduction of the triangular Trapeze line, flaring from the shoulders to a wide hemline just covering the knees.

In 1958, too, Balenciaga introduced his 'Empire' line, and his 'baby doll'; the style named for the short nightdress worn by Carroll Baker's nymphet in the eponymous film based on two Tennessee Williams plays. The film was lambasted by the Legion of Decency: Givenchy's 'baby doll' dress rose above the knee. And in London Mary Quant was designing dresses so short and simple that until now only children would have worn them . . . Change was clearly in the air; and change to an almost unprecedented degree.

Left: Dress and hat from Hattie Carnegie, 1952. Horst's photograph shows off the sharp, tailored lines of an era when Christian Dior said he wanted clothes to be 'constructed like buildings', calling attention to the contours of the female form.

Left: Models posing for one of Christian Dior's last collections, 1957. The range of shapes shown not only reflects the versatility with which he had rung the changes on the silhouette through the preceding decade; it suggests the incipient move towards a less rigorously fitted line. Modern designer duo Viktor & Rolf describe this shot, taken for *Life* magazine, as 'an icon of the great couture era... a dream and an escape from reality.'

Left: Balenciaga cowled velvet robe, photographed at Versailles in 1952. The stand-away collar was one of Balenciaga's favoured style statements, as was the elegant simplicity of shape.

Above: Shantung silk shirt dress, 1955. The full skirt was typical of the decade, as were stylised floral prints in colours too bright ever to be seen in nature.

Following page: Yves Saint Laurent's first collection for the House of Dior in 1958 saw the 21-year old hailed for the 'Trapeze' line, which *Time* magazine described as 'the first big change in female fashions since the New Look', and which heralded some of the radical changes in fashion shortly to come.

*"As Christian Dior,
that most modest of men,
said to me, 'No one person can
change fashion — a big fashion
change imposes itself."*

Carmel Snow

Then & Now

Designers have long-relished the glistening effect of crystal, mirror and metallics – from back in the 1920s, when photographer Lee Miller wore this mirrored dress by Lucien Lelong (facing page), to Dolce and Gabbana's widely-worn belted creation of winter 2007-8 (above). Paco Rabanne made this chain mail dress (above left) in 1967, while Diana Dors' curves appear to best advantage in this shimmering textured dress at the Cannes film festival, 1956.

chapter

TWO

Changes
1959–2008

The sixties saw a seismic shift in fashion, which embraced the drama of the new with futuristic styles. UK fashion designer Sally Tuffin observed that prior to the fifties: 'There weren't clothes for young people at all. One just looked like one's mother.' But all that was set to change and the power of youth culture was acknowledged in what was dubbed the 'youthquake' by American *Vogue*; for the first time it was girls who wore fashion while their mothers lagged behind in a state of conservative shock. (Mind you, back in 1915 one magazine declared that 'In the matter of dress, history teaches that the modes of Fashion have ever reflected the moods of the people...it is for the young that we want fashion nowadays.') Traditional rules of dress, which had operated within fashion for centuries, were discarded. The old concepts of day dresses, cocktail dresses, dinner dresses and ball dresses, along with the archaic diktats related to shoes, gloves and hats, were overthrown. 'There was a time when clothes were a sure sign of a woman's social position and income group', said Mary Quant. 'Not now. Snobbery has gone out of fashion, and in our shops you will find duchesses jostling with typists to buy the same dresses.'

Yves Saint Laurent at Dior highlighted the new mood in 1960 with his 'Beat' collection, which drew inspiration from the street styles of teenagers and included a black crocodile skin, mink-trimmed biker jacket and matching mink-covered crash helmet. He showed that street fashion could be translated into sophisticated and elegant styles, but the fashion press hated it, declaring it was only for the very young. St Laurent looked outwards for inspiration, utilising points of cultural reference as no designer had done before. Some of his most revolutionary work was in separates, notably the tuxedo suit, 'Le Smoking' and safari suits, although, as he pointed out, 'Young people didn't wait for me in order to wear trousers. They had worn them for a long time already when I worked for Dior.'

The mini, one of the biggest revolutions in the history of clothing, was first seen on the catwalk of André Courrèges' 1964 spring collection, but was popularised by young British designers such as Mary Quant and Barbara Hulanicki, who recognised the potential to create high fashion for the masses. Quant points to the mods as the leading influence in women's fashion of the early sixties. Mods opted for a conservative tailored look with an Italian slant. Quant noted: 'It was the mods who gave the dress trade the impetus to break through the fast-moving, breathtaking, uprooting revolution.' The mini was such a powerful fashion statement that it made all other styles look instantly dated. Initially hem lengths were not so eye-poppingly short, though in 1965 a British fashion show of minidresses in Times Square, New York, stopped traffic on Broadway. It was not until 1968–69, when designers were moving into midi and maxi lengths, that miniskirts reached indecent heights.

Previous page: Courrèges' 1964 collection marked fashion's radical move into Sixties modernity. It is interesting to contrast his style with the conservative dress of the audience.

Right: Jean Shrimpton models a Mary Quant dress, 1963. Quant said: 'Once the rich, the Establishment set the fashion. Now it is the inexpensive little dress seen on the girls in the high street…looking, listening, ready to try anything new.'

Interestingly Chanel, who did so much to raise hem lengths in the 1920s, declared the mini to be 'disgusting'.

As the space race got under way and Russian Yuri Gagarin became the first man to orbit the earth in 1961, fashion got caught up in the furore. Designers were highly experimental and innovative in their use of materials: in 1964 Courrèges' white and silver Space Age collection made headlines around the world. It is a look that is used regularly to illustrate the fashion excesses of the sixties, but it was breathtaking in its stark precision and in its use of high-tech metallic fabrics. 'Artifice increased with the space race,' said Vogue. 'Before man landed on the moon, the unwritten rule, which said plastic was for picnics, metal for cutlery and paper for printing on, was thrown out of the window.'

Pierre Cardin and Paco Rabanne were also part of the futuristic movement. They showed plastic disc dresses, creating a new form of body armour. The sharpest dresses were super-short and cut into tubes or triangles; shoulders, waists and bosoms were minimised. Three years after Courrèges' Space Age collection, when Paco Rabanne worked with Jacques Fonteray on costumes for the cult sci-fi film *Barbarella*, the overtly sexual outfits were not a million miles from what could be seen on the streets. The combination of rising skirt lengths, daring cut-outs and blatant transparency served to smash any last notions of an 'acceptable' moral dress code. Sixties' fashion was all about breaking boundaries.

The seventies, popularly regarded as a time of anti-fashion, saw individuality, freedom and choice emerge in fashion terms. Dress was a political statement, whether it was 'peace and love' hippie chic, the dungarees of the feminist, the hot pants of the dolly bird, the anarchic glory of punk, or the shirtwaister uniform of the conformist career woman. British *Vogue* pronounced that 'The real star of the fashion picture is the wearer…you,' and American journalist Tom Wolfe labelled the seventies 'The Me Decade'. The hippy movement, which had reached a high point in San Francisco in 1967, spread around the western world and argued against the seasonal shifts of the fashion industry. Hippies wanted to express their individuality and focus on a style they liked. Vintage fashion moved to the fore, and thrift shops were raided. This marked a turning point in fashion, for prior to this movement vintage – essentially second-hand clothing – had been only for the hard-up.

In fashion terms the seventies advanced the concept of creative dressing, or dressing-up, turning to ethnic cultures and retro styles for inspiration. *The Women's Room* (1977), the book by Marilyn French that epitomised so much about the age, described one character who would turn up 'looking like the princess in a fairy-tale book. She found oddly embroidered blouses, used sari fabric to make something flowing, found strange beads and jewelry with great heavy stones, and wore them all as if they were her native dress.'

Real breakthroughs were made in the field of textile design, with print emerging both as fashion statement and a radical form of self-expression. Emilio Pucci had started the process in the sixties with swirling vibrant designs. In the late sixties designers such as Celia Birtwell, with her partner Ossie Clark, and Zandra Rhodes exploded on to the scene with exquisitely beautiful textile designs that were integral to the overall outfit rather than a mere complement to it. 'I'm a textile designer that couldn't find a job', said Rhodes, 'and went into fashion by accident'. Rhodes took chiffon to a new exotic dimension, She interpreted the kaftan as a graphic shredded chiffon masterpiece, said Australian designer Jenny Kee. 'No one had shredded fabric like this before – Zandra rethought construction – she invented overlocked chiffon and stretched silk jersey with the seams on the outside as frills.'

Kenzo Takada mixed his own bold colourful prints and ethnic influences in flowing shapes when he launched his influential Jungle Jap range in the early seventies. Missoni had a similar impact with his sensual, multi-coloured knitwear.

Vivienne Westwood, although not the creator of punk, is inextricably linked with the unfolding costume drama of this style revolution. She was perhaps the first designer to be so closely associated with street fashion that it is hard to define what grew up from the streets and what she contributed to the overall look. The story was violent, subversive and designed to shock. 'Punk brutality delivered a karate chop to fashion', observed Colin McDowell. 'It destroyed in order to reconstruct and the new ideas it brought reduced the continuation of previous fashion styles to nothing more than decadent recycling.' There were no rules: trashy fabrics and those more commonly associated with the sex industry were worn with tartans and leopard prints; clothes were ripped and torn; zips and safety pins were essential decorative features, along with swastikas, chains and studs. Westwood inevitably

succumbed to the allure of the dress, but her vision was in latex, cut indecently low in the neck and pornographically short in hem.

At the beginning of the 1980s the Japanese designers arrived in Paris and offered women a radically alternative way of dressing. Although entirely different from punk their style similarly challenged conventions. These clothes had no notion of sexuality, luxury or elegance. As with punk, clothing might apparently be ripped, though in fact these tears had been artfully constructed and carefully woven or knitted into the fabric of the garment. The designs of Issey Miyake, Rei Kawakubo of Comme des Garçons and Yohji Yamamoto were the antithesis of seventies' retro and eighties' power dressing. Their asymmetrical cuts and misshapen hemlines combined to produce a body that was layered and wrapped in oversized cuts with a deliberately *unfinished* finish – a ripped dress could cost a small fortune.

A Rei Kawakubo collection caused the look to be dubbed 'post-Hiroshima'. These designs offered a totally different view of femininity, with women dressed as waifs wrapped in asexual layer upon asexual layer of twisted, knotted and sculpted fabrics. Sex appeal was not overt; this is, if you like, feminist fashion. Indeed Kawakubo has said that she designs for strong women who attract men with their minds rather than their bodies. It took the industry time to embrace this new style of dressing. Joan Kaner, Vice-President and Fashion Director at New York store Bergdorf Goodman, complained that 'They do nothing for the figure, and for all the money going into health and fitness, why look like a shopping bag lady?' It helped that the Japanese made the colour

Left: Bold red and white dresses from Andre Courrèges, 1968, highlight his boxy, uncluttered, comfortable style and trademark flat round daisies. He was probably the most plagiarised dress designer of his day.

black avant-garde once more (Rei Kawakubo was said to work in a dozen shades of black), so much so that it became a uniform for artists, writers, journalists and designers for the next ten years. But women embraced the look and dressed in dark, voluminous, loosely belted, multi-layered dresses.

In complete contrast, designers Thierry Mugler and Claude Montana embraced strong, emphatically tailored, dominatrix silhouettes, introducing the notion of power dressing, a look translated by the mighty US soaps *Dallas* and *Dynasty* and embodied by America's then First Lady Nancy Reagan. Dresses were bold, colourful, patterned, ruffled, frilled and bejewelled and beloved by the wealthy New York social set. The Italian designers offered the subtle alternative and made fortunes proving that power dressing could be soft, luxurious, business like and elegant.

The fitness-obsessed eighties saw sports clothes moving to fashion centre stage for the first time. Tunisian designer Azzedine Alaïa created a whole new body-conscious and skintight style of dressing – his thesis is 'The base of all beauty is the body'. His focus was always on the dress, but his complex cut and extravagantly sexual designs revealed an entirely new approach. Alaïa used spiral seams and stretch fabrics to create his figure-hugging frocks, and though dependent on the

Left: Ossie Clark observed that in the late sixties and early seventies the clothes themselves weren't that important. 'It was a whole attitude. It was about girls taking off their bras and enjoying themselves.' Here he embodies the romantic mood in a dress featuring a print by his wife Celia Birtwell, 1971.

toned tautness of the body, the dresses themselves appear sculpted into shape even on the hanger. The style was modified for the high street and women ventured forth in tiny Lycra dresses that were little more than elongated vests.

The biggest fashion change in the nineties was arguably the high fashion reintroduction of colour and print in dresses, starting with browns (the new black in the early nineties) and moving on to Day-Glo and neon brights with plenty of loud prints thrown in for good measure. Nineties dresses evolved from Eighties cling; they were more overt, cut shorter, slashed deeper and appeared in attention-grabbing colour. Versace's bold designs were not for shrinking violets: 'I like to dress egos' said Gianni Versace. 'If you haven't got a big ego, you can forget it'.

Gucci re-established its name with retrospective styles that reworked seventies' classics or offered up-to-date hard, sexy elegance. Similarly Versace produced simple, sexy suits and dresses, so beloved by Diana, Princess of Wales. At the same time sexual fetishism was also big news, from Versace's bondage collection of 1992 to Vivienne Westwood and Jean Paul Gaultier's wilder excesses, dresses were undeniably, ostentatiously erotic.

The inevitable contrast was dresses pared down to extremes of puritanical simplicity. The look was dubbed deconstructionism and was exemplified by the work of Ann Demeulemeester, known as the mistress of minimal and Martin Margiela. As for Japanese designers before them, the construction and shape of the garment was paramount and colours were monochrome or neutral.

'Something that is not obvious looks much more beautiful to me than something that is' says Demeulemeester. 'It is very hard to make something look like nothing.'

The revolution in the noughties could well prove to be the return of the big dress, but without any preconceived fashion rules as to where, when and how. This is the big-time, high-octane, red-carpet approach, a nostalgic return to unadulterated glamour, whether it be in the form of a frock apparently straight out of a costume museum or a sliver of shimmering fabric apparently inspired by Vionnet. It is a look celebrated by John Galliano at Dior who has relished the opportunity to produce virtuoso frocks.

Brides illustrate the new passion for donning a divine dress. Until recently, fabulous bridal frocks were the sole preserve of the young, 'virginal' church bride. Today they are enjoyed by the young and the old, whether single, divorced or heavily pregnant, whether exchanging vows in a cathedral, council buildings, or on the beach – anything goes, from Wang to meringue.

But perhaps no one illustrates the new approach to dressing up better than Naomi Campbell, who on finishing five days of community service in 2007, mopping floors and cleaning toilets in New York, exited the building in style in a crystal-encrusted, metal-corset-belted Dolce & Gabbana siren dress, with no hint of a shamed face.

What might have once been worn to a royal ball might now turn up at a gallery opening; a vampish slip of satin previously intended for a trip to a nightclub could well appear at a suburban dinner party and a pretty fifties style dress can be worn to work. Cult US series *Sex and the City*, arguably started this trend by beaming weekly doses of fantastical high fashion gloss into sitting rooms around the globe. The character of fashion connoisseur Carrie Bradshaw, as embodied by Sarah Jessica Parker, and her friends, Charlotte, Miranda and Samantha, combine to offer a cross-section of dress 'personalities' for the viewing public to emulate. In the terms of this book, you might almost say that Charlotte is feminine, Miranda classic, Samantha sex and Carrie a mix of fantasy and art.

Above: Eighties fashion celebrated luxury and ostentation and produced feminine styles full of pattern, colour, frills and fuss, as in this Emanuel Ungaro collection from 1985.

Opposite: Thierry Mugler embraced strong, emphatically tailored, dominatrix silhouettes, here in 1979, introducing the notion of power dressing; a look translated by the mighty US soaps *Dallas* and *Dynasty*.

Left: Vivienne Westwood's mini-crini, 1989, showed her burgeoning interest in taking details from historical costume and giving them her own subversive twist.

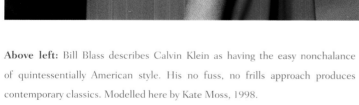

Above left: Bill Blass describes Calvin Klein as having the easy nonchalance of quintessentially American style. His no fuss, no frills approach produces contemporary classics. Modelled here by Kate Moss, 1998.

Above right: 'The sensuality of the body – everything it expresses and the messages it sends – is very important', explains Stefano Gabbana, who, together with Domenico Dolce, designs clothes for real women with hips and breasts. Dolce & Gabbana modelled here by supermodel Cindy Crawford in 1992.

Left: 'The base of all beauty is the body' according to the 'King of Cling', Azzedine Alaïa. His revealing dresses epitomised the high-heeled sexuality of the late-eighties and exposed his theory that there was 'nothing more beautiful than a healthy body dressed in wonderful clothes.' Here, his take on the little black dress, 1990.

Following page: John Galliano marks Christian Dior's 60th anniversary with his haute couture collection for Dior, 2007/2008, shown at the Versailles Castle Orangery. 'My role is that of seducer,' he says.

"I want fashion to be beautiful, escapist, aspirational. Fairy godmothers are hard to come by so let me tell you: you shall go to the ball! Make life more of a fantasy and more of the story you imagined."

John Galliano

Then & Now

The flaring effect of the 'Minaret dress' (top left) created by Erté and Paul Poiret for the play of that name in 1913 is echoed in the ball dresses designed by Charles James and photographed by Cecil Beaton in 1946 (opposite). The dress with the accordion hemline by Pierre Cardin dates from 1973-4 (bottom left), and the concertina sculpture (above right) by Issey Miyake dates from 1994.

chapter THREE
Must Have

Imagine the moment: it's 1930, a fashionable party, eight women suddenly realise that they are wearing the same black silk dress with a necklace of artificial flowers. There were (so legend says) tears, torn fabric, necklaces stamped underfoot...and the new name on the block, Marcel Rochas, was made. Decades later Givenchy told the story of how eight women turned up at a party wearing copies of a striped dress he had made for the Duchess of Windsor: the Duchess burst out laughing and led them all into a conga line.

Fashion has always held a precarious balance between exclusivity and availability. On the one hand, exclusivity was the point of the haute couture industry that flourished for the first half of the twentieth century and whose individually crafted fruits were simply unavailable to the vast majority of women. On the other, if a creation were not worn, or at least craved by that vast majority, then it might be beautiful, but could it, by definition, be fashionable? 'If there is no copying, how are you going to have fashion?' as Coco Chanel asked sagely. Or, as *Harper's Bazaar* put it: 'almost every woman, directly or indirectly, has worn a Balenciaga.' When Wallis Simpson married the Duke of Windsor in June 1937, wearing a blue Mainbocher day dress, *Life* magazine covered the story. Over the months ahead versions of the 'Wally' dress became available at stores ever further down the food chain from Mainbocher's august premises until, six months on, Klein's Cash and Carry sold it for just $8.90.

A new disseminator of individual looks was the cinema. Up until the mid-1920s *Vogue* editors, eyeing the overblown creations seen in the silents, used the term 'pretty Hollywood' to denote vulgarity, but that was soon to change. Hollywood remained content to follow the basic diktats of Paris as to line and style, rather than to innovate. But what it could do was to popularise. Schiaparelli started to design clothes with conspicuously broad shoulders from the very start of the thirties but the look only really took off when, in 1932, the costume designer Adrian (looking for a way to disguise Joan Crawford's boxy shape) gave the star huge ruffled sleeves in *Letty Lynton*. No surprise, perhaps, that it was Schiaparelli who declared: 'the film fashions of today are your fashions of tomorrow'. Macy's (shown the designs in advance by the MGM studio publicists) reputedly sold half a million copies of 'the Letty Lynton dress', and that's to say nothing of all the women who ran up copies for themselves. Adrian's prediction that 'the movies would become America's Paris' was on the way to being fulfilled.

In an article in *Motion Picture Studio Insider* Adrian warned fans: 'Don't copy the screen costumes you see exactly, because they are often too 'stagey' for the average woman's wear'. He showed how he would modify one of his Joan Crawford creations into something suitable 'for the average girl to copy'. Though several costume directors, Adrian among them, went on to work in consumer fashion, in their screen work they were

Previous page: The Little Black Dress, here from Hattie Carnegie, is the ultimate 'Must Have'. As *Vogue* put it in 1944: 'Ten out of ten women have one – but ten out of ten want another because a little black dress leads the best-rounded life'.

Right: The 1950s were characterised by the circular-skirted, bright-coloured look and further exemplified by the sherbet-coloured confection that was the prom dress, still familiar from movies such as *Grease*.

Above: 'Utility' fashions from 1943, designed by Norman Hartnell for Berketex,
show the boxy shapes and masculine influences of the war years. Accessories and
detailing were often used to cheer an austere and economical basic design.

marching to a different drummer. They were governed by the need to hide the flaws of a particular actress; to tell a story; to make an impact in only a few minutes of screen time; and of course to come up with a design that would 'read' in black and white. All the same, Travis Banton, visiting London in 1937, found duplicates of the clothes he had recently designed for Carole Lombard in *Rhumba* in the window of one of the most fashionable stores.

Even period films had their effect on twentieth-century costume, such as the 'Mary sleeves' named after the designs Walter Plunkett made for *Mary of Scotland* (1936); or the Elizabethan ruffles that studio staffers took from the wardrobe department to fancy up their little black dress.

The war years, in a sense, saw the ultimate 'must-have' in the shape of government-ordained clothing: the frock or suit that in Britain was called 'Utility', in America 'Victory', and in Germany 'Everyman's'. If this was essentially a different fashion imperative – fashion by decree, rather than by desire – it is nonetheless true that the no-nonsense look matched the mood of the times. The years after the war have been dubbed the golden age of couture, but just as important was the pressing imperative of the *prêt-a-porter* or ready-to-wear market.

From the 1930s more and more women, first in America and then in Europe, had been able to buy dresses 'ready-to-wear'. In the inter-war years, couturiers had once fought against the ever-present copyists who sold inferior versions of their frocks at a fraction of the price. But gradually a more realistic attitude was creeping in: 'if you can't beat them, join them.' By Christian Dior's day, a

couture house sold, firstly, made-to-measure garments to private clients and, secondly, models to commercial buyers who would copy them for wider distribution. By 1957, when Dior died, his couture house had already become a business empire making everything from perfume to ties, with a number of other companies turning out Dior goods under franchise. But then Dior was one of the most commercially astute of designers, the one who early decided to promote his own designs in the USA, subtly altered to suit the American market. (He was also one of the first to employ a publicist. By contrast, when Dior's contemporary Balenciaga heard a journalist was coming, he hid. Guess which name is known to a wider audience today?)

Sears mail order and *Vogue* patterns all helped to spread the message. As the great original ideas became part of the Zeitgeist they were popularised in both senses of the word: the swirling skirts of Dior's New Look became, a decade later, the circle skirt of the American teenager.

America produced the first great designer whose revolutionary designs began life as 'must-haves'. Claire McCardell began her career with the mass-market, casual-wear-oriented Townley Frocks. It was there that she made (purely for her own use, and based on an Algerian costume) a bias-cut, street-length tent of a garment, apparently shapeless until the wearer belted it around her waist. A buyer spotted it, ordered 100, and ran an advert on a Sunday in September 1938. By Monday afternoon the buyer had ordered another 200, and the 'Monastic' dress was born. Five years later McCardell's 'Popover' dress – a wraparound blue denim coverall created at the request of *Harper's Bazaar* for a generation of wartime women having to do their own housework for the first time – sold 75,000 copies within the year. What's more, it showed no sign of dying when the year – or the war – ended. Many of us are still wearing McCardell designs today.

It's tempting to make a link between McCardell (and Chanel before her) and Mary Quant: the female revolutionaries who have made fashion easier for women, when male designers have sometimes seemed to make it more demanding. 'The whole point of fashion is to make fashionable clothes available to everyone,' Quant said.

Mary Quant opened her first shop, Bazaar, in London's Chelsea, in 1955. She had not planned to produce her own range, but when she was unable to find what she wanted Quant set about learning pattern-cutting. In 1962 Quant won a lucrative contract with the US chain store J.C. Penney, and in 1963 took her range into mass production with the Ginger Group in the UK. Her look was essentially light-hearted and user-friendly. It was Quant and not Courrèges who made the mini the 'must-have' hem length of the sixties, though she herself said:

> It wasn't me or Courrèges who invented the mini-skirt anyway – it was the girls in the street who did it. London led the way to changing the focus of fashion from the establishment to the young. As a country we were aware of the potential of these clothes long before the Americans or the French.

In America Jackie Kennedy appeared in *Life* magazine wearing a brightly coloured shift dress designed by an old school classmate, one Lilly Pulitzer. Her dresses, which had hitherto been worn only by Hampton or Palm Beach society ladies, became a national obsession and the popularity of the look was quickly picked up by manufacturers across America and Europe. There was hardly a woman or child in the sixties who did not own a version of the simple, colourful Pulitzer shift. *Ladies Home Journal* noted that: 'Jackie's slightest fashion whim triggers seismic tremors up and down Seventh Avenue.'

In 1969 Dior's chief designer Marc Bohan observed that since skirts could hardly get any shorter they would have to get longer. Even *Life* magazine joined the debate in March 1970 with a cover article on 'The Great Hemline Hassle'. Women were torn: the mini was perceived as 'young fashion', while longer hemlines were regarded as dowdy in comparison. Men were firmly pro-mini: in the USA, the Associated Press reported on the existence of defiant groups such as the 'Ban the Midi' club. The controversy is one that in the long run finally helped push women into trousers. It has been estimated that in 1971, in France alone, the number of women's trousers sold jumped from eleven to fourteen million, while the number of dresses dropped from eighteen to fifteen million. Certainly the seventies saw trousers being accepted for the first time for work and formal wear, where previously they had been strictly casual.

Barbara Hulanicki founded Biba in 1963, originally as a mail-order business. She recalls:

> I got a call from Felicity Green at the *Daily Mirror*, who wanted a dress for her pages. She asked me what the company was called and I remember thinking, 'Oh my God, I have no

idea.' So I named it Biba after my little sister. I designed a gingham dress with a matching headscarf, inspired by the dress Brigitte Bardot wore when she married Jacques Charrier. We received 17,000 orders for that dress, all by post.

Hulanicki and her husband, Fitz, were not keen on opening a shop, but they moved into an old chemist's shop on Abingdon Road in Kensington, London, for use as an office. One Saturday Barbara left the door open and the shop filled with girls. They walked in and were buying the only thing in the shop – a one-size brown pin-striped smock. Hulanicki remembers: 'I rang Fitz and he brought more smocks.' The smock dress sold in shed loads during the sixties and early seventies.

The first Biba shop opened in 1964, with evocative art nouveau interiors and clothes hung on basic bentwood coat hangers. Biba was incredibly cheap and it was possible to buy a new wardrobe without worrying about the cost. Clothes were cleared as fast as they hit the shop floor. The Biba label became a must-have in its own right for ten years, for Hulanicki had her finger firmly on the fashion pulse. Her style was consciously feminine, featuring strong colours and prints on dresses with tiny armholes, puffed sleeves, teardrop collars, flared hems and lines and lines of buttons. By the Seventies Hulanicki's style had evolved into emphatic 30's vamp. The excitement generated was legendary and women all over the country wanted to travel to London to visit Biba. Biba's customers included Bardot, Twiggy and Julie Christie. Twiggy, who wore a Biba dress to her sister's wedding in October 1965, recalls her dress with perfect clarity:

It was A-line with a tight top and little armholes, and short for the time, two inches above the knee. It was a primrose yellow background with a pink one inch chevron pattern in a zigzag. It was one of Barbara's polka dot, zigzag and gingham phases. It had a high neck and puff sleeves to the elbow, very Biba. Three round pearl buttons at the neck. It was a great dress.

'As time went on', explains Hulanicki, 'we had to move every two years because each shop became too small.' In 1973 they transformed the old Derry & Toms department store on Kensington High Street to offer Biba fans the whole lifestyle experience. This attracted visitors by the thousand, but it was to witness the environment rather than to buy and in 1975 the store closed and Biba came to an end (though the label has recently been revived). Biba originals have since acquired cult status in the vintage market.

Laura Ashley created some of the most popular fashions in the 1970s, though her statement was somewhat anti-fashion. Ashley's designs fulfilled the dream of the romantic, pastoral idyll. She started in textiles – Heals and Liberty were among her early clients – and she moved into clothing partly by accident after a few gardening overalls were snapped up as dresses in 1961. Ashley extended her range, and her plain and floral-sprigged cotton pinafore dresses marked the nostalgic mood of the seventies. They became a runaway success, and her company achieved a multi-million-pound turnover. By the mid-1970s Ashley was selling in Europe, Canada, Australia and the USA and the public could not get enough of her look.

Left: In America Jackie Kennedy appeared in *Life* magazine wearing a brightly coloured shift dress designed by an old school classmate, one Lilly Pulitzer. By the end of the sixties there was hardly a woman, teenager or little girl who did not own a version of the simple, colourful Pulitzer shift. Here the young matrons of Palm Beach wear original Lilly Pullitzer designs in 1964.

On a similar theme, crafted clothing imports from the East were immensely popular, complementing the hippy ideal by utilising ethnic clothing to make a political statement. The voluminous kaftan was adopted across the world as the height of cool. Such was the public enthusiasm that designers rapidly created their own more streamlined, pared down, stylish versions: Halston used silk jersey; Thea Porter, Gina Fratini and Zandra Rhodes turned to lightweight silk chiffons covered in exotic prints or frills. The look became de rigueur as casual eveningwear and was seen everywhere, from Hollywood to New York's Studio 54 to suburban dinner parties. Elizabeth Taylor, Marisa Berenson and the Beatles were all keen kaftan wearers.

The Diane von Furstenberg wrap dress was launched in 1973 and caused an immediate sensation. The advertising tag line was: 'Feel like a woman. Wear a dress!' It was a look that meant business yet one that still projected a feminine image and it offered a viable alternative to the unisex look adopted by most professional women. By November 1976 sales of the dress had topped five million and von Furstenberg was dubbed by *Newsweek* the most marketable woman in fashion since Coco Chanel. The secret of the dress was, and is, that it is flattering to both young and old alike. The look has enjoyed an enormous surge in popularity more recently, with vintage dresses being dusted down. In 1997 von Furstenberg launched a new generation of wrap dresses, sparking a buying frenzy that resulted in a rush of chain-store copies. Her admirers range from Candice Bergen and Betty Ford to Gloria Steinem, Jade Jagger, Kylie Minogue and Madonna.

The dress itself, though always present within fashion ranges, did not hold quite the same 'must-have' status in

Above: Rachel Weisz shows the allure of a Roland Mouret dress at the premiere of *The Constant Gardener*, 2005. Mouret explained the concept thus: 'There is a new body-shape in the air; we're saying goodbye to the cigarette skinny, size-zero look. Clothes without waists are very androgynous; but once you mark the waist, you give a kind of pinch to an outfit and make it womanly.'

Right: Laura Ashley was hugely influential in the sixties, seventies and eighties with printed florals that provided escapist fantasy for romantic girls. Despite her anti-fashion philosophy feminists were less than enthusiastic about her frilly, feminine fantasies. Designer Helen Storey observed: 'A Laura Ashley smock, which spells the subservient woman locked prettily in her place is far more frightening than black plastic boots.'

the eighties and early nineties. Power suits, jeans, tracksuits and slogan T-shirts all took turns to dominate, although some of Gucci's and Versace's result-wear dresses were obligatory evening wear for bright young things. Accessories are the must-have purchase of the new millennium, with

> *"Feel like a woman.*
> *Wear a dress!"*
> Diane von Furstenberg,
> advertising tag line

Left: Diane von Furstenberg launched her wrap dress in 1973, a design that looked like it meant business yet still projected a feminine image, as displayed here by Cybill Sheppard, accompanied by Robert De Niro, in *Taxi Driver*. By 1976 sales had topped five million and Furstenberg was dubbed the most marketable woman in fashion since Coco Chanel by *Newsweek*.

designer shoes and, most notably, handbags acquiring cult status and generating massive waiting lists. In the noughties your clothes can come from value outlets so long as you have the obligatory designer accessory.

However, 2005 saw a change in mood, and von Furstenberg was not the only designer to enjoy the resurgence of the dress. Roland Mouret showed his 'Galaxy' dress, designed to make women look like fifties Hollywood starlets. The look was old-time glamour, the dress made with a complex construction and cut to bring out what one wearer called 'a whole new womanly you'. In this dress you stood differently, walked differently and men behaved differently towards you. The look was so hot that every famous name appeared in it, including Scarlett Johannson, Rachel Weisz and Victoria Beckham. No one seemed to care that it had been seen before. Two years later Mouret's 'Moon' dress, in figure-hugging stretch cotton, had the same effect: despite a £990 price tag, shops were selling out within hours of receiving new stock. Deeply glamorous and gloriously flattering, it celebrates the female body – and can only be worn with towering heels.

That Mouret's stunning 'Galaxy' dress bears a startling resemblance to a Dior day dress from 1956 merely proves the point that many must-have pieces are timeless. Celia Birtwell's prints are back in the high-street after a thirty-year absence from the fashion scene, and Pucci and Missoni are as fashionable today as they were fifty years ago. Some dresses have a fashion personality so distinct that they survive long after their moment has passed.

Of course, one 'must-have' dress has never gone out of style. Perhaps it never will do. In 1926 Coco Chanel presented a long-sleeved black crêpe dress which *Vogue* likened to the model T Ford and said would become 'a uniform for all women of taste'. Historically the colour of death (and of power – because to produce black fabric took such a quantity of expensive dye), black had become the colour of servants and of the mourning, the unhappy. There is also an element of perversion in its sexuality. If black has found its own significance for every generation since Chanel's – from the intellectuals of the Paris Left Bank to the Goths of London, and reborn as the uniform of the working woman in the early eighties – the little black dress, or LBD, has shown almost as much versatility.

The LBD was (in a more than usually sexy incarnation) the dress that made Elizabeth Hurley; and it was what Diana, Princess of Wales, chose to wear on the evening her estranged husband was making his televised bid for popularity. Every designer has done an LBD, from Balenciaga to Claire McCardell, from Armani to Lagerfeld. Black – and the little black dress – can be the ultimate non-statement, but the LBD can also be the garment that speaks most clearly. As *Vogue* put it in 1944: 'Ten out of ten women have one – but ten out of ten want another because a little black dress leads the best-rounded life. Is a complete chameleon about moods and times and places. Has the highest potential chic (only if well-handled). Has the longest open season.' In 1951 *Woman and Beauty* told its readers: 'Invest your all in one good little black dress.' The advice hasn't changed today.

Right: A mixture of bold colour and geometric print combined on simple shift dresses characterises the dramatic, Op Art influenced designs of the late sixties.

Right: The sleeves Joan Crawford sported in the 1932 film *Letty Lynton* sparked a flood of imitations – even though costume designer Adrian's original goal had been merely to disguise Crawford's broad shoulders.

Opposite: Claire McCardell, 1946. McCardell's simple, timeless designs were heavily influenced by sportswear and the demands of the outdoor life.

The Little Black Dress

> "*Scheherazade is easy. A little black dress is difficult.*"
>
> Coco Chanel

Below: Coco Chanel – original creator of the wardrobe staple 'The Little Black Dress' – is seen in the later stages of her career, adjusting a model's frock.

Left: Model Marion Morehouse wears a Chanel dress from 1926.

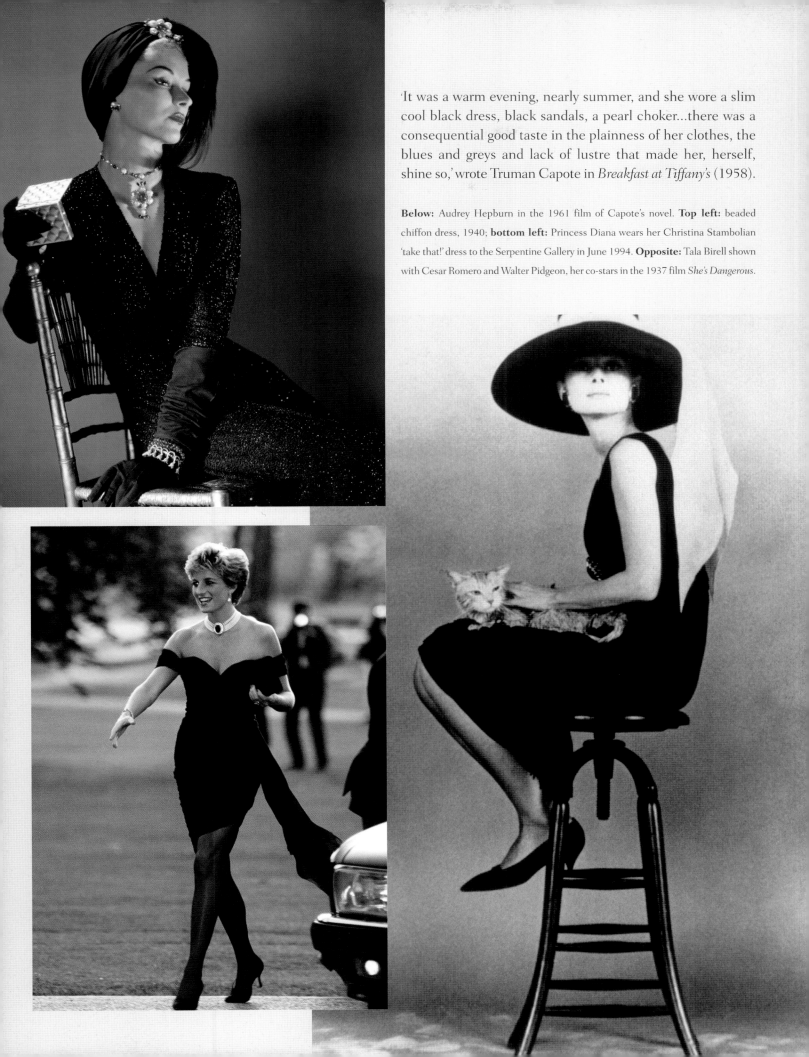

'It was a warm evening, nearly summer, and she wore a slim cool black dress, black sandals, a pearl choker...there was a consequential good taste in the plainness of her clothes, the blues and greys and lack of lustre that made her, herself, shine so,' wrote Truman Capote in *Breakfast at Tiffany's* (1958).

Below: Audrey Hepburn in the 1961 film of Capote's novel. **Top left:** beaded chiffon dress, 1940; **bottom left:** Princess Diana wears her Christina Stambolian 'take that!' dress to the Serpentine Gallery in June 1994. **Opposite:** Tala Birell shown with Cesar Romero and Walter Pidgeon, her co-stars in the 1937 film *She's Dangerous*.

chapter
FOUR
Classical

A renewed interest in the aesthetics of the classical world signals – so it has been said – that we are entering a new era of self-invention. On the whole, the world of fashion bears out this theory. Certainly the revolutionary political changes at the end of the eighteenth century had been signalled by the classically-based Empire look, and the dramatic social changes of the early twentieth century saw the style come round again.

But it's worth saying here that almost every designer – even the least likely – has had his or her classical moment. An exhibition on the female classical form at New York's Metropolitan Museum of Art in 2003 – under the banner 'Goddess' – juxtaposed recent Prada dresses with those by the far more obvious Madame Grès half a century before. Schiaparelli, giving it a theatrical twist, could pose a model in pure pale drapes against a pillar and a giant picture frame. Even Versace costumed the models for one *Vogue* spread in little lamé tunics, like something in an orgiastic Greek fantasy. More seriously, the sexuality for which Versace is famed is often (not always) based on following the lines of the body in a simple and essentially classical way.

It may be necessary later to make a distinction – and, conversely, to trace the connections – between classical, in its literal sense of relating to the ancient world, and classic, defined by the dictionary as 'of the highest class...serving as a standard or model of its kind...adhering to an established set of principles characterised by simplicity, balance, regularity, and purity of form'. But for the first decades of the twentieth century the visual influence of the Graeco-Roman world was so direct it is tempting not to look

beyond it. And indeed, it is arguable that a 'classic' style of dress became an interesting concept only in subsequent years, in counterpoise to a youthful and iconoclastic alternative.

In the early part of the century, Paul Poiret and Jeanne Paquin both used the Hellenic style, with muslin and light silk hanging off the shoulders to move loosely around the body. Copies of Mariano Fortuny's many-pleated 'Delphos' dress, inspired by ancient Greece and with pleats made by his own special process, not only continued to be worn by their proud possessors almost half a century after he made the first version in 1907, but live on today in their influence on Issey Miyake. Fortuny's sleeveless tunics, caught at the waist with a knotted cord, were echoed in Claire McCardell's 'Monastic' dress of 1938, just as shades of Madeleine Vionnet and Madame Grès can be seen in the modern work not only of Miyake, but of Rei Kawakubo and Junya Watanabe. When the miniskirt came in, historians pointed out that this look had last been seen on the Greek girl athletes.

The fashion historian Colin McDowell wrote in *Fashion Today* that, 'If anyone can be distinguished for inventing twentieth-century fashion for women, it is Madeleine Vionnet' – because it was Vionnet who gave women the confidence to accept their bodies. Vionnet, whose first salon opened before the First World War, and who like Fortuny took her inspiration from the garments of the ancient Greeks, famously cut fabric on the bias, so that the diagonal line continued to swirl around the body. In her early days she caused a furore by insisting that her designs should be shown on a naked model.

'I have tried all my life to be the physician of the figure – I wanted to impose on my clients a respect for their bodies,' she said. In recent decades, comparisons have been made between Vionnet and American designer Geoffrey Beene; but though Azzedine Alaïa's reputation as the 'King of Cling' hardly seems to make him Vionnet's most obvious heir, it is perhaps he who – dressing the toned bodies of the 1980s – has followed her most closely.

Vionnet said that: 'One must examine the anatomy of every customer. The dress must not hang on the body but follow its lines. It must accompany its wearer and when a woman smiles the dress must smile with her.' She called herself 'an enemy of fashion. There is something superficial and volatile about the seasonal and elusive whims of fashion which offend my sense of beauty.' She was certainly no friend to the dictatorship sought by some designers. There should, she said, be as many fashions as there were types of women.

By the same token Madame Grès – 'the eminence Grès' – also had the reputation of being indifferent to what other designers were doing. Grès (whose salon Alix opened in 1931) was informed by the early twentieth-century interest in sport for women. The dancer Isadora Duncan had been her muse. 'If the bias [cut] of Madeleine Vionnet underlines the body, the drapes of Grès exalt the movement,' wrote Grès' biographer Laurence Benaim.

Grès' garments were usually white, or in what she called the *'faux blancs'* – 'the colours of Crete and of light'. She draped jersey straight onto the body, and loved artificial silks and the light new fabrics, which she claimed gave a

> "*Never fit a dress to the body but train the body to fit the dress.*"
> Elsa Schiaparelli

dress the line that the fabric itself wanted to have. Though they called her *'l'Hellène de Paris'*, a leading exponent of the French neo-classical style, Grès herself claimed never to have been inspired by antiquity. *'Le rétro'*, she said, 'does not interest me. It is the future *qui me passione.'*

Perhaps its affinity with the body – trying though it can be for those whose bodies are less than perfect – explains why the classical look also had its influence on Hollywood. Alongside the sexual suggestiveness of the dresses of Hollywood's golden age can be seen, paradoxically, a strand of classical elegance. Long clean lines worked best on screen, and reflected the strength of icons like Dietrich and Garbo. The classical dresses Katherine Hepburn wore in *The Philadelphia Story* (1940)

not only express, as film costumes must do, the keynotes of the character – who is compared to a Greek goddess – but also sparked a sales boom for the designer who provided one stunning gown. Adrian, the Hollywood costume designer turned couturier, would make evening gowns like columns, decorated in Greek designs.

The forties saw dresses based on the Roman toga, often made from new lightweight materials – but this tubular shift worked as a shape for the fabric-starved war years because it didn't use too much fabric of any kind. Frank Perls, the art dealer who in 1953 sponsored a retrospective exhibition of Claire McCardell's work, described the first McCardell dress he ever saw as being 'the eternal dress straight from the Acropolis...all clean cut, nothing made up...nothing stuck on.' What he was describing was at once the classically-derived and the 'classic' style.

Perhaps the direct 'classical' influence becomes harder to trace in the 1950s. But the decade that saw the dawn of youth fashion – American teenagers wore puffy prom dresses and swirling skirts ornamented in bold motifs – saw also frocks that were tailored to an almost austere purity of line. By the same token the sixties, so aggressively modern and directional, would not appear to

be a time for 'classical' design to succeed. But in fact it crept in with a glorious inevitability. The utterly basic sixties' shift dress is a perfect evocation of classical design: even coloured sugar pink or covered in sequins, the pure lines still shine through.

Hubert de Givenchy, whose elegant and beautifully cut clothes were to become a byword for timeless elegance, perfectly epitomises the new classical lines of the sixties. His designs for Audrey Hepburn in *Breakfast at Tiffany's* in 1961 (even though it was Edith Head and not he who was credited) have made her probably the ultimate style icon of the last fifty years. Film director Billy Wilder had already declared that 'This girl may single-handedly make bosoms a thing of the past.' Hepburn's look was quintessentially different from the voluptuous feminine ideals of the fifties and marked the look of the new decade.

American designers were the key exponents of this new movement. First Lady Jackie Kennedy, who was never going to follow fashion slavishly, was nevertheless hugely influential on fashion throughout the world. An overview of her wardrobe shows a woman of immense personal style and confidence, who had the courage to dress with the utmost simplicity and refinement; sleeveless A-line dresses became a personal signature. She was initially criticised by *Women's Wear Daily* for her 'Francophile' fashions, but subsequently did much for home-grown talent. She wrote to Diana Vreeland for advice: 'I must start to buy American clothes and have it known where I buy them'. She worked extensively with Oleg Cassini, asking him to dress her as if Jack were the President of France. Designers like Norman Norell, with his comfortable silhouettes and easy glamour, or Oscar de la Renta with his sophisticated, grown-up and svelte style, maintained the tradition.

Most women had slavishly attempted to follow fashion until the seventies – even Queen Elizabeth was seen in an above-the-knee dress and boots in the sixties – but the wild excesses of seventies' fashion forced a rethink. There really was very little that women beyond the age of forty – thirty even – could, or would want to, wear. A former editor of British Vogue, Ailsa Garland, in her book *Lion's Share* (1970), highlights the problem: 'Freddie Grisewood asked me about miniskirts and I told him that Norman Hartnell had one day said to me that he thought they were a mistake on the whole as most women had knees "like rock cakes, dear".'

Best remembered for retro styling, glam rock and some of the more spectacular theatrical fashion statements, the seventies nevertheless saw real developments in producing modern clothes of perfect and pure design, with styles that quietly changed the way we all dress.

Moreover, any woman interested in pursuing a serious career faced a genuine dilemma, either they dressed like a frumpish matron – remember Margaret Thatcher? – or they followed fashion and got overlooked for promotion. There came a point where fashion was alienating a large percentage of a lucrative client base.

It was essential that a new style of fashion developed to satisfy the demands of the modern woman, and the purity of classical styles provided the inspiration. The contribution of the classic designers to womenswear should never be underestimated: they succeeded in quietly shifting conventions in dressing. Their clothes did not dominate; they were soft, unpretentious and perennially modern in their simplicity.

In the UK Jean Muir made her mark with stylish and understated dresses that didn't date. The American designer Geoffrey Beene moved the concept on with his own fluid garments. His clothes are elegant, but sporty and relaxed at the same time. He gave the term classical a new contemporary attitude.

New York designer Halston dressed some of the most stylish women of the decade; Jackie Kennedy, Babe Paley and Bianca Jagger were devotees, Diana Vreeland and Andy Warhol were admirers. His elegant clothes were an antidote to fussy dressing and his pared-down style is characterised by lean or billowing jersey columns and simple tailored shirt-dresses. He is generally regarded as the forerunner of designer sportswear. His style was effortlessly modern, soft and unconstructed and suitable for women of all ages and sizes. Tom Ford, designer at Gucci, acknowledged Halston's Studio 54 look – bold, fluid columns – as a precursor to nineties' style.

Calvin Klein has a reputation for knowing what women want to wear and has followed the path of no-fuss no-frills design. The simple shirtwaister was one of his first dress styles. *Time* magazine defined him as 'the true American puritan'. 'I like clothes that slide when the body moves,' Klein observed. 'I couldn't design a pouf (puffball) if you put a gun to my head.' His clothes are both intensely practical and luxurious, and the look is

Left: 'I am interested in dressing modern American women' says Calvin Klein. He experienced a renaissance in the nineties, offering a backlash against eighties vulgarity. He believes that repetition is reputation and returns to the same themes again and again in search of perfection, here from 2008.

Right: 'The essence of style', says Giorgio Armani, 'is a simple way of saying something complex'. He regards discretion as the enemy of vulgarity. Here Giorgio Armani puts his philosophy into practice, 1999.

what Bill Blass describes as 'the easy nonchalance of quintessentially American style'.

Italian designers also began to make their presence felt in the ready-to-wear market in the mid-seventies. From the first their clothes tended to be classically cut but innovative, and beautifully made from the finest Italian textiles. Armani in particular established a reputation for soft, deconstructed cutting. His clothes are deceptively simple: the cut beautiful and the fabric, whether matt crêpe or slippery satin, allowed to speak for itself. His womenswear made its mark in the late seventies and the Armani suit changed the way women dressed for work once and for all.

This is when the term 'classic' began to be heavily used. It has been downgraded by journalists, and used by some retailers to describe their least adventurous line. But it ought instead to suggest a piece of outstanding design. Modern design 'classics' are elegant, practical and comfortable – the very essence of classical style.

Donna Karan, who launched her first collection in New York in 1985, is a case in point. As with Halston and Klein, her streamlined, flattering and practical designs are contemporary, but they have real staying power.

They have a strength and simplicity that ensures longevity: they become wardrobe staples that can be worn twenty years hence with pride.

In the 1990s designers such as Helmut Lang and Jil Sander joined established names in developing a signature of smart, elegant and contemporary design. It would be a mistake, however, to think that only certain designers produce classic styles. Any designer with a multi-million pound/dollar/euro turnover will be savvy enough to recognise that what grabs press attention and raises the profile will not necessarily sell. All designers will turn out classic designs when the mood or the muse takes them, even the more surprising candidates such as Versace – or Jean Paul Gaultier, who designed the simple black dress that Nicole Kidman wore to the 2003 Academy Awards.

It is a mark of the significance of classic design that the women who wear it frequently appear on the 'best dressed' lists. The clothes have a quiet assurance, a million miles away from result dressing or attention-grabbing theatricals; they do not dominate, but are calming, soothing, reassuring to both wearer and onlooker; the epitome of good taste and personal style.

"The dress must not hang on the body but follow its lines. It must accompany its wearer and when a woman smiles the dress must smile with her." Vionnet

Previous page: The thirties heyday of classical style is exemplified by these Vionnet dresses from the start of the decade; while (**Right:**) the 1936 evening dress by Madame Grés ('Alix') show the use of fabric that made her the queen of classical drapery. 'If the bias [cut] of Madeleine Vionnet underlines the body, the drapes of Grès exalt the movement,' wrote Grès' biographer Laurence Benaim.

Opposite: Halston's evening dresses were unpretentious and elegant, he called them his 'Goddess' gowns. Here Beverly Johnson, the first black model to appear on the cover of *Vogue*, models Halston in 1975.

Above: Halston was the first American designer celebrity. He defined American style with comfortable, understated casual clothes in expensive and luxurious fabrics. His credo was 'You are only as good as the people you dress' and he attracted a huge celebrity clientele. Here a billowing jersey dress from 1978.

Left: Claire McCardell's dress of 1946 is photographed in a pose that suggests the Statue of Liberty. 'We specialize in what we like best, in what satisfies us most deeply. For me, it is American, what looks and feels like America', McCardell said. 'It's freedom, it's democracy, it's casualness, it's good health. Clothes can say all that.'

"Her style came from a deep well of substance... She transformed the American sense of style." Frank Rigg

Left: Jacqueline Kennedy shows off the contemporary elegance of an Oleg Cassini gown on a trip to Mexico City with JFK in June 1962.

Following page, left: Marion Morehouse (wife of the poet e.e. cummings) wears a two-tone sheath dress with a two-layered hemline from Callot Soeurs, 1924.

Following page, right: Amber Valetta models Gianni Versace's colourful take on the classical look, 1995. Although he is associated with decadently sexual dresses, many of Versace's designs are pure, classical pieces of design, perhaps shaken up with a sprinkling of gaudy colours or shimmering detail.

Above: Claudia Schiffer in pleated silk from Chanel's 1992 couture collection.

Left: Lebanese designer Elie Saab is known for turning women into modern day goddesses: 'Classic elegance is wearing something that fits and highlights the beauty of a woman's curves and shape. It is also refusing to be a fashion victim,' says Saab. His designs are favoured by European royalty and feature regularly on the red carpet, here a classical piece of drapery from his 2007/08 couture collection.

Above: Scarlett Johansson could compete with Helen of Troy in this silk satin Stella McCartney dress worn to the London premiere of *The Other Boleyn Girl*, 2008.

chapter FIVE Fantasy

There is no hard-and-fast dividing line between those dresses that seem born of pure fantasy – the desire to be somewhere else in place, in time, in reality – and the influential, here-and-now, cutting edge of fashion. Christian Dior said of his 1947 New Look that: 'Girls could safely feel that they had all the trappings of a fairy-tale princess'; couturiers, he claimed, 'embody one of the last refuges of the fabulous'. Designers early realised that what they were selling was not just a garment, but a mood, an illusion – a fantasy. The couturier Lucile (Lady Duff Gordon – sister, appropriately, to the legendary romantic novelist Elinor Glyn) is often credited with having introduced the idea of giving each dress a name, such as 'the Sighing Sound of Lips Unsatisfied'. But it was Poiret who was revolutionary in commissioning an album of fashion illustration by Paul Iribe, *Les Robes de Paul Poiret, racontées par Paul Iribe*. Later, of course, the work of the great photographers echoes the same theme: every picture tells a story.

More directly, the dresses of the early decades of the century showed the influence of the Ballets Russes, of South Sea paintings and the vogue for all things oriental. The discovery of Tutankhamun's tomb in 1922 prompted a crop of Egyptian motifs. Even Chanel in the early twenties might add a Russian style fur trim to a tunic, influenced by the flood of Russian émigrés who came to Paris after the Russian revolution (or, more specifically, by her affair with the Russian Grand Duke Dmitri). One cannot but think of Yves Saint Laurent's 1976 'Russian Revolution' half a century on; and the whole inter-war 'peasant look', as *Vogue* called it – Balkan embroideries, Schiaparelli's knitwear based on Armenian designs – prefigured the fantasies of much later in the century.

The past has been another source to plunder, and of course many of the classically-inspired dresses discussed in the last chapter themselves represent a kind of fantasy. Fortuny, living in Venice, found himself also inspired by the velvets of the sixteenth century. Norman Hartnell's use of symbolism in the dresses he made for Queen Elizabeth II echoes the embroidered devices on the dresses of another Queen Elizabeth, in the sixteenth century. (Eyes and ears, in the Hatfield 'Rainbow' portrait, to signify that the mighty Bess saw and heard everything that went on in her kingdom…it's an idea that could have come from Schiaparelli's Surrealist phase.)

Hollywood too was a purveyor of fantasy. Female audiences lusted after the $3,500 dress worn (for only a few minutes) by Dietrich in *Angel* in 1937 – jewel-encrusted, sable-bordered, a solid figure-hugging column of sparkling embroidery – and the red bugle-beaded dress created by Adrian for Joan Crawford in 1937, so extravagant it weighed an impossible 35lb (16 kilograms). Women saw the hostess gowns of the thirties' Hollywood films (or of the film star caught 'at home' in the fan magazines) and many brought themselves to believe that they too might entertain in velvet and ostrich feathers, a garment halfway between an evening gown and a nightgown.

Though the costumes of the period epics might seem to have little to do with the dresses of everyday reality, they reflected the preoccupations and preconceptions of their own era. One such epic, *Marie Antoinette* (1938), sourced authentic silks and laces in Paris; when the same star, Norma Shearer, made *Romeo and Juliet* (1936), historical costume expert Oliver Messel had been brought in to design the dresses. A set of alternative designs was also prepared, at the star's request, by Adrian, one of Hollywood's own; no prizes for guessing which proved to be more appropriate for the camera!

By contrast, the crinolines in *Gone With the Wind* had an oddly symbiotic relationship with the trend real-life fashion was taking at the time. As *Vogue* wrote in October 1938, only months before the film came out, 'Make no mistake, you'll be wearing, as a matter of course, clothes that a year ago would have seemed pure fancy dress, notably crinolines, authentic hoops, strapless bodices, bustle backs…You may have one *à la Eugénie* or a Victorian – but have one you must; they are truly contemporary.' Though the trend went into temporary abeyance during the war, it reappeared afterwards. The famous corset scene in *Gone With the Wind* is curiously reminiscent of Pathé newsreel footage of models donning the underwear that went beneath Dior's New Look.

Dior evoked the feminised glamour of his mother's age (and of Madame de Pompadour's, and that of the widely commemorated Empress Eugénie) in the same way as the designers of the 1970s did the pastorals of an earlier century. The ballerina-look of the post-war years, with flat slippers under full skirts and hair drawn smoothly back, itself represented a fantastical look backwards to early Victorian days. The echoes of Velázquez's paintings in Balenciaga's designs had an element of fantasy as surely as did Vivienne Westwood's conscious evocation of the era of Watteau. But it is no coincidence that most of the dresses in this section come from the last part of the twentieth century. Is it fair to say that the historical inspiration of the early designers was so clearly secondary

> ## "*If you can't be elegant, at least be extravagant!*"
> ## Moschino

to their own vision that later generations surely 'borrowed' more crudely? Or is it just that we, today, fail to recognise the elements of fantasy in a time from which everything seems fantastical to us?

In 1964 fantasy took a futuristic turn. André Courrèges, Pierre Cardin and Emanuel Ungaro, inspired by the space race and sci-fi visuals, created innovative designs that used the newest fabrics and fastenings. This was a gloriously naive view of the future, but Courrèges' minimalist designs caused *Women's Wear Daily* to dub him 'the Le Corbusier of fashion'. Total dedication to the complete 'look' was required; the startling accessories included sculpted peaked caps and domed helmets that were worn along with flat shoes, boots and gloves.

1967 saw flower power take over from modernism; in 1969 the Woodstock festival took the message to the world. The singer and writer George Melly declared that 'The hippy revolution killed the Swinging London image'.

The freewheeling Californian ideal sold the notion of nonconformity on a giant scale, a social and political movement that fashion merely served to reflect. Dresses lost ground as the dominant garment, swept away in a tidal wave of granny skirts, jeans and peasant blouses.

In 1968 fashion journalist Bridget Keenan wrote in Nova magazine: 'Fashion is experiencing one of the most interesting dilemmas of its history. There is a state of anarchy.' The young distanced themselves from conventional fashion, choosing instead to express concepts of free thinking, peace and love through their dress. In the same year *Women's Wear Daily* wrote that: 'To find a personal expression of beauty one has to search the soul.' There was a growing nostalgia for the past and disenchantment with the futuristic modernism.

Echoing the mood, Yves Saint Laurent took inspiration from around the globe; indeed some of his best-known and most influential collections have their roots in other cultures. His 1967 'Africa' collection was perhaps the first to show real commitment to an ethnic theme. He utilised wooden and glass beads, plastic appliqué, raffia and

Left: Zandra Rhodes' designs, 1970. 'A Zandra frock can take a horsey aristocrat and transform her into a gorgeous wood nymph. A Zandra frock can take a hard boiled Hollywood agent and make her into a bohemian glamour puss." Simon Doonan, author and Creative Director, Barneys.

Page 97: A fantasy from Christian Lacroix's haute couture collection,1999. 'The forward looking/backward looking nature of fashion is indisputable' observed Christian Lacroix, 'although it is rarely mentioned as one of the *raisons d'être* of a discipline that claims to be brand new every season.'

ebony and ivory jewellery. The collection was so complete a story and so modern and ahead of its time that the fashion press was stunned – forty years on his cocktail dresses, a mass of flesh-revealing beadwork, are still dazzlingly contemporary. What Saint Laurent did with this and other collections was to look at the history of traditional costume and, for the first time, translate it into lush, ornate and glamorous fashions; Rifat Ozbek would do the same in the eighties.

Designers began to cherry-pick influences, with no regard to cultural strictures or historical accuracy. In the early seventies Kenzo, who was inspired by national dress, mixed international influences, initially drawing heavily on his Japanese roots. He combined strong colours and prints in joyous dresses that caught the mood of the era. Similarly Bill Gibb combined prints and borders in vast, tent-like dresses, the sheer volume of which had not previously been seen outside maternity departments.

Zandra Rhodes used voluminous shapes to display her extraordinarily beautiful signature prints. These dresses concealed rather than revealed, they highlighted the beauty of cloth, print and colour rather than the body beneath it. They hinted at bohemian leanings, artistic sensibilities and a repression of western values, combining visual fragility with implied strength of character.

The flip side of the coin was the emergence of retro styles ranging from thirties' vamp to milkmaid. Laura Ashley reacted against the formal decrees of fashion, producing cotton frocks in traditional floral patterns. This was the soft-focus take on the rural idyll, the rosy-cheeked milkmaid, all frothy white petticoats and soft floral prints; it was pure dressing-up, not so much feminine as juvenile. If this was a political statement it would have hinted at tradition and conformity – nice girls didn't wear boldly printed kaftans, paint flowers on their cheeks or proclaim women's rights, they donned Laura Ashley pinafore dresses and looked fresh, lovely and unthreatening. Biba offered a worldlier alternative, with glamorous thirties-style dresses in dark smudgy colours, echoing the dangerous mood of the 1967 film *Bonnie and Clyde*.

Ralph Lauren recognised the importance of American heritage and looked to his own country for inspiration. His runaway success was in selling a nostalgic lifestyle, whether it be the twenties' fashions seen in his hugely influential costumes for *The Great Gatsby* (1974), or in his early-1980s frontier dresses, which made women want to dress as though they had just stepped out from the prairies. He sold the American dream back to the American people and on to the rest of the world. However, unlike Laura Ashley he moved with the decades and was focused on reality when designing, claiming that he was motivated by considering how his wife and daughter wanted to dress.

Karl Lagerfeld at Chloé, who was hailed by the *Los Angeles Times* as 'the new idea man of the seventies', showed extravagant retrospective creations, whose titles alone highlight the fantasy involved. The 1975 Shepherdess dresses and the swashbuckling salute to pre-Revolutionary France of 1977 were hugely admired by press and buyers alike. Lagerfeld told *Vogue*, 'If you don't have humour you don't have much,' and he has used wit both in his own collections and also to spectacularly turn

around the profile and profits of the house of Chanel, which he took over in 1982.

In London the high camp of seventies' glam rock, giving way to the hard edge of punk, had taken the concept of dressing-up to new heights. Street fashion became massively influential and the city became a magnet for designers from around the world. Vivienne Westwood moved on from the excesses of punk: her 1981 'Pirates' collection was the ultimate New Romantics look. In 1982 she showed satin bras over sweatshirts, but from 1983 she moved away from street styles to more whimsical interpretations of costume, producing the mini-crini, which in turn gave birth to the puffball and bubble skirts. Some of her dresses appear to be beautiful reinterpretations of period costume.

Elizabeth Wilson, in *Adorned in Dreams*, writes that: 'This obsession with pastiche, this "nostalgia mode" is related to the way in which the dictatorship of haute couture broke down in the 1960s and 1970s. A single style can no longer dominate in the post-modern period. Instead there is a constant attempt to recreate atmosphere. In the fantasy culture of the 1980s', she wrote in 1985, 'there is no real history, no real past; it is replaced by an instant, magical nostalgia, a strangely *unmotivated* appropriation of the past.'

Right: British model Twiggy, who defined the look of the sixties, planned to give up modelling for acting with the film *The Boyfriend*. 'if this film was a success, please God I could give up modelling for ever. I was really sick of it. I didn't want to be a clothes horse any more.' Twiggy wore this specially designed Bill Gibb 'peasant' dress to the premiere of Ken Russell's film in 1970.

Christian Lacroix plunders various cultures as well as history for influence, pointing out in his book *On Fashion* that the series of exotic influences that fashion has soaked up throughout the last hundred years 'have transformed the way we dress into a tangible map of the world'. His style is marked by a bold mix of lush fabric, print, embroidery and trim combined in dramatic shapes. He took the puffball and turned it into a trademark pouf. Nevertheless his theatrical designs had broad appeal and could be worn by New York's social X-Rays, royalty – Sarah Ferguson, Duchess of York – or even a pop princess: Christina Aguilera opted for Lacroix on her wedding day in 2005.

John Galliano took the concept of fantasy one step further. He told fantastic stories with each collection: fashion historian Colin McDowell describes him as the Hans Christian Andersen of fashion. 'Above all I want fashion to be beautiful, escapist, aspirational', says Galliano himself. 'Fairy godmothers are hard to come by so let me tell you: you shall go to the ball! Make life more of a fantasy and more of the story you imagined.' Galliano's prolific talent was given full rein when he was made design director of Dior in 1996.

Jean Paul Gaultier challenges notions of conventional good taste, mixing it with a hefty dose of wit. His moniker, *'enfant terrible'*, hints at his wild streak. In 1983 he despatched a model down the catwalk in a beautiful velvet dress with sculptured conical breasts, as Yves Saint Laurent had done before him; but what was entirely unacceptable in 1967 was now adopted as an ingenious style statement and political comment. The look was championed by Madonna in her 'Blonde Ambition' tour.

The ultimate fantasy dress, one of the best-known frocks of the century, is Princess Diana's wedding dress. Interestingly enough the style is not so far removed from that of another iconic fairytale princess, Snow White. It had a sweetheart neckline, puffed sleeves and vast skirt and was made from 45 feet (14 metres) of ivory silk taffeta, decorated with 10,000 mother-of-pearl sequins and pearls with a 25-feet (7.5-metre) train. Anna Harvey of *Vogue* observed: 'It was beautiful fabric, stunning, but to Joe Public it looked as though it was made of creased brown paper. The Emanuels admit that they had underestimated the effects of the train being squashed into the cramped coach.' However, a copy was available in London's West End the following day and the 'meringue' style, as it became known, is still immensely popular. 'We had all seen a wagonload of brides in white before we saw her: after her, every white-clad bride seems to be Diana, in all her doomed glory,' wrote Julie Burchill.

Fantasy may be about shock value, the desire for a designer's client to stand out from the crowd and to make a fearless style statement. But it can also be about fulfilling romantic daydreams – costumes for grown-ups.

Left: Ethnic trends were important in the seventies and everyone wore a kaftan from the Beatles to Elizabeth Taylor: here a chiffon kaftan with gold thread by Andre Oliver for Pierre Cardin, 1973.

"*I love old things. Modern things are so cold. I need things that have lived.*" Barbara Hulanicki

Right: Designer Ossie Clarke described Biba as offering: 'Disposable glamour shrouded in purply, mulberry shades.' Biba creator Barbara Hulanicki produced designs that were slightly decadent, yet reasonably priced, here a black and silver sequinned dress from1969.

Following pages: John Galliano was inspired by Symbolist painters for his big-volume, jewel-coloured intricately embroidered collection for Dior, 2008.

Above: Swashbuckling drama from Vivienne Westwood, who takes historic garments and reinvents them, here from 2006/2007. Westwood herself explains: 'I do believe that my clothes are a criticism of mediocrity and orthodoxy.'

Right: Alexander McQueen uses the juxtaposition of romantic and contemporary elements to produce ethereal sculpture with this tattered ivory silk chiffon and silk organza 'oyster' dress from 2003. *Women's Wear Daily* noted: 'The clothes are better up close, revealing a mind boggling degree of creativity and of work.'

Right: Yves St Laurent's 'Africa' collection of 1967 was perhaps the first designer collection to show real commitment to an ethnic story. His designs are startlingly ahead of their day and featured in his final haute couture show of 2002 which included a retrospective of his work.

Opposite: The glowing colours and heavy jewellery of these 1940 gowns suggest the self-conscious glamour and conceptual orientalism of Hollywood costume.

Wedding Dress

'Diana was not just a bride, she was *The Bride*', wrote Julia Burchill. But before and after Lady Diana Spencer's wedding to Prince Charles in 1981 (see over), the bride was and ever will be a figure of fantasy. Grace Kelly similarly carried with her the dreams of millions when she married Prince Rainier of Monaco on April 19, 1956, in a dress created by the Hollywood costume designer Helen Rose (opposite). Elizabeth Taylor's first ever wedding dress, for her wedding to Nicky Hilton on May 6, 1950, was also designed by Helen Rose (bottom left). It was very similar to the dress Taylor wore in the film *Father of the Bride*, which was released shortly after her nuptials. Galliano created this fairytale wedding dress for Gwen Stefani in 2002 (top left). Edwina Mountbatten in her wedding dress, 1922 (above).

chapter
SIX
Sex

The purpose of clothing, wrote the surrealist Salvador Dali, is to 'Hide… Protect… Provoke!' He called costumes 'a constant metaphor of the erogenous zones'. The 'Spine' dress Elsa Schiaparelli made in 1945, after almost a decade of collaboration with Dali, could be worn only by the bravest even today. Almost invisible among the intricate folds of the black silk crêpe lies a zip directly over the pubic region, its metal teeth declared to represent the *vagina dentata*. Perhaps the first thing to say when discussing the provocative content of dresses is that the modern age by no means has it all its own way. Lucien Lelong made a dress with a bra on the outside as far back as the 1930s. Jean Paul Gaultier's famous – or infamous – conical breasts of the mid-eighties had been seen almost twenty years before (and in even more conspicuous eight-inch projections) in Yves Saint Laurent's 'Africa' collection of 1967, though it cannot be said that they were received enthusiastically.

Sex, you might say, depends on surprise. It wasn't that Elizabeth Hurley showed so much flesh in Versace's famous safety-pin dress – it was that the gaps of bare skin between the black fabric appeared so unexpectedly. And when Katharine Hamnett showed a model whose dress

Previous page: The famous see-through dress designed by Yves St Laurent, 1968. It caused a sensation and marked the start of a new kind of overtly sexual fashion statement.

Right: Rita Hayworth in *Gilda* (1946), a film dominated by the dangerous power of seduction, and one which made the actress into the ultimate femme fatale. 'Every man I knew', Hayworth said once, 'had fallen in love with Gilda and wakened with me.'

blew up to reveal tights over an otherwise nude crotch, it was far more shocking than simple nudity would have been. Half a century earlier, Paul Gallico wrote in his fantasia *Flowers for Mrs Harris* of a Dior dress – the aptly named 'Temptation' – made of jet-encrusted black velvet, frothed at the top with cream, white and delicate pink. 'The garment covered Natasha most decently and morally and yet was wholly indecent and overwhelmingly alluring.' Exactly.

The great fashion historian James Laver elaborated the concept of the shifting erogenous zone, whereby as one area of exposure loses its capacity to shock and thus its appeal, the wheel of fashion inevitably rolls on to focus on another part of the body. It's hard, today, to recreate the frisson that must have been felt when hemlines first began to rise in the 1920s, making it permissible for a woman to show a (rouged) knee for the first time in modern history. And if the new flapper skirts were presented more in terms of physical and political independence than of allure (a woman's ability to do without a man, as much as her ability to attract one), well, the sexual message has often been all the more insidious for not being spoken directly.

Poiret's hobble skirt of a slightly earlier period appeared to echo the erotically-charged constraints of bondage gear, of a geisha's teetering walk or a Chinese woman's bound feet. It also, of course, made the elitist point that the wearer had no need, as well as now no freedom, to engage in any kind of manual work. 'I have freed the bust from its prison, but I have put chains on the legs,' Poiret said. But in fact, hidden pleats or even slits in the skirt permitted more movement than might at first appear possible.

By the same token, there is a hidden story behind the 1930s' invention of the back as fashion's new erogenous zone, displayed in a deep reverse décolleté, pointed up by a strategically placed flower or a necklace of pearls worn behind. The move to display the spine, and to draw attention to the arms with elaborate sleeves, came in part from the new sunbathing cult, and the Health and Beauty movement. But the new great populariser of trends, Hollywood, also had its part to play. In the early years of film, actresses had been expected to display far more on screen than would ever have been allowed on the street. But from the early 1930s the Hays Code imposed strict regulations on what was and was not allowed in American motion pictures. Every gown had to pass the censors and designers had to find new, less obvious, methods of sexual invitation. The code laid down precisely how much of the cleavage could be seen at the front – but said nothing about the back. Nothing about a heavily draped cowl neck drawing attention to what it concealed, nothing about removing the bra underneath the covering fabric and nothing about how tightly the fabric clung to the lines of thigh and stomach. Vionnet's 1920s discovery of the bias cut, with its unprecedented ability to make satin cling to the figure, paved the way for the slinky film-star gowns that came to epitomise the sex-appeal of the era. They are still potent (and still worn on the red carpet) today.

Left: Liz Hurley accompanies Hugh Grant to the premiere of *Four Weddings and a Funeral* in 1994 in a Versace kilt-pin dress. Photographer Richard Young had been warned by the Versace PR team to expect 'something pretty out of the ordinary... The dress did everyone a lot of good. That picture made the front pages of newspapers worldwide.' *Women's Wear Daily* described Hurley as 'a woman who came to the public's attention in a couple of pieces of cloth and safety pins'.

The sexuality of the post-war dresses, like those of the Edwardian age half a century before, lay in the way they emphasised and exaggerated the curves of the female form. In Dior's New Look the appearance could be overtly decorous, but hidden padding increased the jut of the hips and made the waist look smaller by comparison. By the start of the 1950s Dior was showing an alternative line of dresses and costumes, rigorously ladylike in their all-covering formality, but so skin tight that the bones of a model's pelvic girdle could be seen; around the same time Balenciaga's individualistic new cuts revealed the unexpected appeal of hitherto unregarded erogenous zones like the neck or the wrist, displayed by a stand-away collar or a bracelet-length sleeve.

The sixties were a time of sexual revolution: contraception became more widely available to women, married or not, and it was inevitable that fashions would reflect the dramatic social changes. Their sexual significance was that for the first time in history women were showing off their thighs. The older generation was scandalised by these provocatively short hem lengths, but in fact the mini was curiously asexual. The dresses themselves were demure, figure-concealing and childlike in design; or rigid and formal, almost like futuristic sculptures. The message was more modern woman than sex kitten. Indeed it was Twiggy's androgynous figure and innocent face that made her *the* model of the decade.

Mary Quant's husband, Alexander Plunket Greene, commented on the look in *Rolling Stone* magazine in 1987: 'People were very shocked by the clothes, which seem so demure and simple now. At the time they seemed outrageous. I think there was a slightly sort of

"Now we feel there is nothing wrong with dressing ourselves as a prostitute, provided that this costume is chosen with deliberate humour and irony."
Tama Janowitz

paedophile thing about it, wasn't there?' He observed that the fashionable woman of the fifties, 'all high heels and rock-hard tits', was overtaken by a girl with a childish shape and a great deal of long leg. 'Which was all pure erotic fantasy...a bit of Nabokov I suppose.'

The most overtly sexual story to emerge from the decade was transparency. In 1965 see-through dresses appeared for the first time outside of a revue and by the end of the decade Saint Laurent was sending out silk chiffon evening dresses with the merest fluff of ostrich feathers circling the hips for decency. This was a notional boon for heterosexual men, though in reality the average woman drew the line at revealing her breasts, even though she thought little of wearing the shortest of hem lengths.

Fashion wallowed in nostalgia through the seventies, but punk heralded another small-scale revolution at the tail end of the decade, with bondage clothing (for both men and women) utilising the materials of the sex shop – latex and nylon. Clothes fit for a brothel and designed for shock value were more threatening than sensual: they were designed to challenge the system and the status quo. Vivienne Westwood and Malcolm McLaren started the trend, selling bondage clothing from their shop SEX in London's King's Road. Their shop assistant Jordan, sheathed in latex dresses, embodied the style as celebrated in Derek Jarman's 1977 film *Jubilee*.

Zandra Rhodes, inspired by the dramatic punk looks, created beautifully made silk jersey evening dresses featuring perfectly stitched holes held together with jewelled safety pins – a look that resurfaced more than a decade later in the Versace dress worn by Elizabeth Hurley to the premier of *Four Weddings and a Funeral*, a dress that turned Hurley into a star overnight. It marked the move into a more body-conscious era – all possibilities were there after transparency had been accepted in the sixties and punk pushed out the sexual boundaries in the seventies.

Tailoring moved to extremes and by the eighties the female silhouette was a parody of the Amazonian dominatrix, with outsize shoulders, pointed breasts and tight waists. Dresses and suits with vast padded shoulders epitomise the early stages of power dressing. Yuppies (young urban professionals) flaunted their wealth and TV soaps such as *Dallas* and *Dynasty* sold the look to women at home, with figure-hugging day dresses topped by mighty shoulder pads. Women were like comic book superheroes, teetering on high heels, and conspicuous consumption was the ethos. Unlike the fashions of the previous two decades, this was not a look strictly for the young. The soaps spread the message that the older woman could have as much, if not more, dangerous sexual allure than the twenty-year-old. The designs of Thierry Mugler and Claude Montana exemplified this smart 'don't mess with me' attitude. Cut and tailoring were stern, dominant and authoritative. Montana said that his inspiration came from the female designers Madame Grès and Vionnet, whose lines were simple, but who exaggerated the female silhouette; however, his look was despised by feminists as a parody of womanhood.

Body consciousness and fitness, a massive eighties' trend, was at the heart of fashion in this decade. Such overt emphasis on the body was a first: until this time clothes had concealed or delineated the body, but with the introduction of Lycra – a beautiful, new, genuinely elastic fabric – it was the body itself that dictated the ultimate silhouette of the dress. The look was not underpinned with corsets as the fifties' sheaths had been. Stretch was the key: designers such as Azzedine Alaïa, the 'King of Cling', utilised the new fabrics to reveal the body in figure-hugging lines.

Right: 'In a feat worthy of literature, Versace seized the streetwalker's bravado and conspicuous wardrobe, along with her blatant, brandished sexuality, and introduced them to high fashion', commented Richard Martin, then Curator of the Costume Institute of the Metropolitan Museum, New York. Here, leather, chiffon and flesh from Versace, 1998.

"Vulgarity is a very important ingredient in life. I am a great believer in vulgarity — if it's got vitality. A little bad taste is like a nice splash of paprika. We all need a splash of bad taste — it's hearty, it's physical…No taste is what I am against."

Diana Vreeland

Westwood and Gaultier both played with sexuality in dress and were the main advocates of the concept of underwear as outerwear. Gaultier's conical breasts and lace-up corset dresses and Westwood's dramatically low-cut and constricting corset dresses, which left breasts exposed like ice cream spilling over the top of a cornet, were initially shocking, yet were massively influential for over a decade. The fact that Yves Saint Laurent had showed off underwear as outerwear in a collection nearly two decades before Westwood and Gaultier made the look their own merely proves that fashion evolution is more gradual than it initially appears – society, not designers, dictates the acceptable face of fashion.

In the nineties, designers such as Versace and Tom Ford for Gucci pushed the sexual boundaries even further, with the trend for dresses with S&M overtones. Fashion historian Colin McDowell in *Dressed to Kill* noted that Nineties women 'wear the trappings of S&M and bondage with the same authority as they were worn by the punks who first brought them out of the sexual twilight'.

Versace's marriage of sex and celebrity made fashion newsworthy in a way it hadn't been for decades. Fashion journalist Hilary Alexander commented after Versace's death in 1997 that 'He virtually single-handedly invented the supermodel' – and he was not afraid to maximise their curves. The fact that a Versace frock on a regular person might look less drop-dead gorgeous (and more overtly sexual) did not serve to dent consumer enthusiasm for his brand of showy ostentation. His consumers bought the sexual myth. 'I wouldn't say the Versace woman is predatory. I would say she is seductive', said his sister and successor Donatella Versace recently. 'Women need to seduce in order to achieve their goals. I don't just mean seduce men ...'

Dolce & Gabbana similarly sell a sexy image, overlaid with hints of fetishism tied in with nostalgia for their Italian roots. Some of their most high-profile dresses have been black, featuring corsetry cuts and satin and lace panels; their designs are beloved by such style icons as Madonna. In the noughties female empowerment is deemed to come from being overtly sexual. Suggestive music videos from the likes of Britney Spears, Christina Aguilera and Rhianna encourage little girls to ape their questionable style. The 'family-oriented' Victoria Beckham dresses like an S&M mistress, and wholesome Kylie slips into an incredibly revealing cobweb by Julien Macdonald. The body is all, starved to skeletal thinness and topped by a pair of fake breasts – but women appear to be eager participants in a cartoon-like vision of female sexuality, in what columnist Ariel Levy terms a 'raunch culture'.

Left: Missoni's figure-hugging feather light knits, originally shown in the sixties, remain perennial favourites. In the first ever show in 1966 Rosita Missoni instructed models to remove their bras because they ruined the line of the clothes.

Previous page: Jean Paul Gaultier's iconic, conical-bra dresses are undeniably and ostentatiously erotic, and a personal trademark that has featured in collections for more than twenty years. Shown here in a 2006 retrospective.

Right: Felix Dennis, one of the men behind *Oz* magazine explained the impact the mini had on men in 1968: 'Women were walking down the street in mini-skirts, in what looked like their underwear. It was almost too much for anyone to stand.' Here Jane Birkin reveals exactly why men loved the mini, c.1972.

Right: There is something almost indecent about exposing the back down to the kidneys and beyond, for it offers a tantalising glimpse of near nudity. Here Gianni Versace shows just how daring it can be, 1993.

Opposite: 1930s evening dresses often explored the allure of unexpected erogenous zones, such as arms, shoulders or spine. This photograph seems to borrow the imagery of the Hollywood vamp to suggest a wanton, dangerous appeal.

Right: Naomi Campbell in 2002 in a typically high-voltage, barely-there design by Julien MacDonald, sometimes known as 'The King of Glamour'. His show-stopping dresses are beloved by celebrities and always cause a stir on the red carpet: Kylie Minogue, Kelly Brook, Geri Halliwell and Paris Hilton are all enthusiasts.

Opposite: Gisele Bündchen, in a side-laced satin dress by Dolce & Gabbana from 2003, exposes the overtly sexual face of fashion. Novelist Tama Janowitz explains the thinking: 'Now we feel there is nothing wrong with dressing ourselves as a prostitute, provided that this costume is chosen with deliberate humour and irony.'

Left: Plastic and satin from Gianni Versace, 1995. UK designer Christopher Kane is a great admirer of his design: 'What has me hooked about Versace is the strong, sexual, elegant and sophisticated predator-woman that it seems to embody.'

Right: In Altman's 1995 film *Prêt à Porter* Thierry Mugler expounded his theory on dress: 'It's all about looking good and helping the silhouette ... and it's all about getting a good fuck honey.' Here Jerry Hall proves his point in a Mugler sequinned evening dress from the same year.

Monroe

Lana Turner might have been known as 'the sweater girl', but one Hollywood actress above all others has to be particularly associated with the dress. The clinging lines suited Monroe wonderfully and she knew it – swimwear apart, it's comparatively rare to see her photographed in anything else. Her clothes sometimes caused outrage but more often admiration. Norman Mailer called her the 'sweet angel of sex'.

On the facing page, the twenties styles by Orry-Kelly she wore in *Some Like it Hot* (1959) provoked the comment: 'like Jello on springs'. The dresses she wore in *Niagara* (1953) were cut so low 'you can see her knees'. When she shot the grating scene from *The Seven Year Itch* (left) in 1954, huge crowds gathered to watch in what should have been a deserted New York street, and the unwelcome publicity helped end her relationship with Joe DiMaggio. The dress she wore (following page) to sing 'Happy Birthday Mr President' to JFK in 1962 provoked politician Adlai Stevenson's famous tribute.

"It was just skin and beads – only I didn't see the beads!"

Adlai Stevenson

chapter SEVEN *Feminine*

It is perhaps only in the last few decades that the dress has been associated with conscious femininity – before that it was merely what women wore. When the twenties' flapper made her bid for emancipation, her cropped head with its *'garçonne'* cut sat above what was, effectively, just a shorter, simpler dress than before. Perhaps it is no coincidence that a disproportionate number of the dresses in this chapter date from the fifties, an era when women, having tasted the freedom of the war years – and often having worn the trousers too – were being asked to confine themselves to home and marriage once again.

The irony is that 'femininity', in this context, means restraint. Designer Helen Storey said once that: 'A Laura Ashley smock, which spells the subservient woman locked prettily in her place, is far more frightening than black plastic boots.' By the same token, the 'feminine' dress often, though not always, implies some constricting exaggeration of the female form. The photographer Bill Cunningham said of Charles James, who for several decades across the middle of the century created a series of monumentally feminine ball gowns, that 'he presented women with a shape that was not their own…the equivalent of someone from the Renaissance who made ceremonial armor.' A dubious compliment perhaps, but it's impossible to dislike the dresses, however you feel about the 'feminine' theory.

Of course, one can't be too pontifical about dates. The complaint that women had begun to dress like men is one that has occurred with monotonous regularity throughout the centuries. In particular, the years between the two world wars had seen considerable debate about femininity itself, and the question of the 'womanly woman'. In the 1930s a strain of intensely feminine dressing – the floating evening dress, the 'Ascot frock' – ran alongside the sharp-suited look that *Vogue* described as 'hard-hearted chic'. World War II itself, like other periods of conflict before it, saw a trend towards a more masculine and indeed military style of female dress.

All the same, it's fair to say that the 'fashion-conscious fifties' – the era of Balmain, Dior and Fath – were perhaps the last great heyday of the dress: the last period when a lady might be expected to have a different dress for every occasion. A Paris collection might run the stately chronological progress of *'robes d'après-midi habillées, robes de cocktail, robes demi-soir, robes du soir courtes, robes du soir, robes à danser, robes du soir longues, robes grand soir, robes de gala'*. The show ended, tellingly, on the *'robe de mariée'*. But in truth the death knell had already sounded for the dress's total dominance of the fashion scene: Hardy Amies declared that while a woman might choose a fantastical dress to wear of an evening, come the day she would reach for a suit, that 'livery for living'.

But the talismanic appeal of the feminine dress will not go away. This, after all, is what Justine Picardie was talking about when in *My Mother's Wedding Dress: The Life and Afterlife of Clothes* she wrote that: 'There has to be a first dress, like a first kiss; there has to be. Mine was the one that my mother made for me to wear to my birthday party: a fairy dress, sewn of translucent net, with matching wings and a glittery silver wand. I was three…' She described the vintage frocks she bought from the market as a student in Cambridge: 'a frilly rose-pink sixties' dress – layered, like petals, its pastel sweetness sabotaged by the fact that it was almost

> ## "The return to femininity reflected in fashion has nothing to do with wearing ruffles..."
> Tina Chow

indecently short...I also bought fifties' cotton frocks – splashed with flowers, vivid pinks and greens, daisies running riot...and a long tulle ball gown, sherbet-lemony skirts cascading from its tightly fitted waist.'

Prom dresses in the fifties and sixties marked a significant rite of passage, since for many young women it was their first 'adult' social event. The overt femininity of these formal gowns emphasises the move that was being made from girlhood into womanhood. These saccharine frocks, all frills, ruffles and lace, were decorously cut to resemble truncated, sherbet-coloured, bridal gowns.

The frothy, girlish femininity of prom dresses highlights the problem many women face when selecting a dress. Realistically, plain, classic dresses look best on the very slender and the well groomed. Sexy dresses or the wilder fashion excesses are simply not desirable for every occasion. But the only alternative route – dressing in 'feminine' style – has somehow become the most daunting option. The comfortable uniform of unisex dressing has left women unused to the feel and flow of feminine clothes. Moreover, softness and frills can feel dangerously submissive. The great irony is that feminine designs are probably the most flattering, and with a gentleness in cut and fabric they mark the glamorous middle ground between sex and purity.

From the 1960s onwards feminine dressing has been focused on evening wear, with two notable exceptions:

Biba's nostalgic, thirties-style print dresses from the sixties and seventies, and Diane von Furstenberg's jersey wrap dress from the seventies and nineties, are demonstrably pretty and unchallenging, as well as being comfortable and practical. They can be worn whatever your age, your height or your haircut. Both were runaway successes because of their common selling points: secure, feminine fashion. Von Furstenberg created the wrap dress in 1973 as an alternative to the unisex look. It was her firm belief that woman could mean business and still project femininity and chic. Marisa Berenson, an acclaimed beauty and von Furstenberg admirer, observed: 'It is fabulous to be a woman because no matter how much we achieve, regardless of how many ladders we climb, we are still women and we get to celebrate our femininity by dressing up.'

Similarly, in 1997 John Galliano summed up the mood of the moment when he took over at Dior and produced the slip dress, a piece of bias-cut satin, trimmed with lace. Reminiscent of evocative film-star lingerie from the thirties, the slip dress was a look that women felt comfortable with. It was pretty and alluring and the high street was soon awash with copies. Feminine dressing is a quietly confident style. As a look it attracts peer approval, for it is equally acceptable to both sexes, whereas fantasy dressing can be directly challenging, and overt sexuality uncomfortably provocative.

Feminine fabrics – lace, chiffon, organza, satin and silk – can transform the purest classic design into a feminine one, as can prints. Emilio Pucci created prints that used

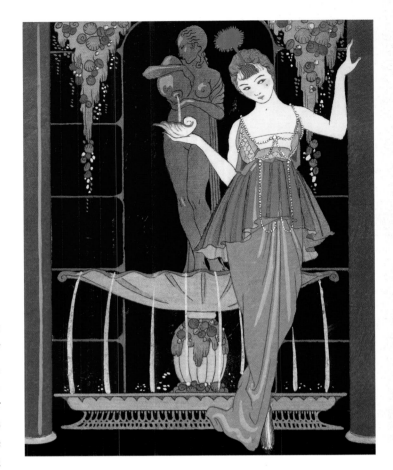

swirling patterns in fantastic colour combinations. The mood matched that of the psychedelic sixties perfectly and Pucci's designs were worn by the likes of Grace Kelly, Elizabeth Taylor, Marilyn Monroe and Lauren Bacall. Missoni created multi-coloured cobweb-fine knitwear that is as popular now as it was in the seventies. Designs from both labels have gone on to become valuable classics. Like the fifties' floral frock they make a statement, but it is foremost one of femininity for, with the occasional exception, men do not relish wearing bold prints or fine gauge knits.

In a world where women are, arguably, most comfortable dressed in trousers, feminine dressing needs to be understated. In the eighties Romeo Gigli showed a new vision of modern femininity that offered a complete contrast to the hard edges of power dressing. His inspiration came from history and non-European cultures, yet his designs are never overblown, overstated or theatrical. His beautifully romantic, floating, day and evening dresses, comprising layers of muted chiffons, reintroduced the concept of femininity to the female wardrobe. Gigli was canny enough to steer away from girlish colours and to avoid frills or fussy detailing.

The British Royal family specialise in feminine dressing – for better or worse. The Princesses Elizabeth and Margaret were both seduced by Dior's New Look, and the Queen Mother floated through life encased in chiffon and feathery accessories. Princess Diana turned herself into a style icon with a succession of fabulous evening gowns. Two dresses mark her style transformation over a thirteen-year period. The first was a full-skirted black

Right: A Georges Barbier illustration from the *Gazette du Bon Ton*, showing a Paquin evening dress, 1914. While the lines of this dress suggest the wings of a butterfly, the 1913 illustration (**Above**), *La Fontaine de Coquillages*, has the fantastical appeal of an aquarium exotic, besides displaying the extravagant forms femininity could take in the pre-war years.

Page 143: Cristobal Balenciaga's lovely floral evening dress, 1952, creates a frame for the model's neck and shoulders. Balenciaga's clients were extraordinarily loyal to a man whose clothes flattered them like no other's.

evening gown worn on her first official engagement in 1981, designed by Elizabeth and David Emanuel and famously unsuitable both because of its colour (royals only wear black for mourning) and its low neck. The second was Christina Stambolian's womanly black lace frock with floating panels worn by Diana to the Serpentine Gallery in June 1994, three years after she had purchased it, on the night her husband confessed to adultery on the television. The dress indicated that Diana was no longer hidebound by royal protocol.

Today, the feminine dress is often defined by a significant event. For most women it's a wedding dress or a party dress, worn when they want to look at their loveliest. But the media is also an important purveyor of the whole

glamour story, and the red-carpet dress is, perhaps, a more significant choice for today's film star than her wedding dress. Her gown will be ruthlessly assessed by the professional fashion commentators and the amateur pundits at home. Her worth will be evaluated: get it right and her profile and dollar value will rise. In 2001 Julia Roberts famously collected her Oscar for *Erin Brockovich* in vintage Valentino, a choice that put vintage back on the fashion map.

The Academy Awards are the ultimate inspirational 'frock' event: stars want to look quietly sexy, while retaining a glamorous edge. No one wants to be dominated by a dress, nor do they want to look too simply dressed; the purest classical evening dresses are best suited to the slim, the commandingly powerful or the ruinously beautiful. Fantasy dresses can be a little OTT: think Björk in the infamous swan dress at the 2001 Oscars. Who wants to be pilloried by the press or to be cited on 'worst dressed' lists, even if you maintain, as she does, that the dress was intended to be a joke?

The red-carpet trauma perfectly illustrates how hard it is to strike precisely the right note in a frock. Dresses, unlike most other articles of clothing, can all too easily tip into extremes. Wallis Simpson is arguably a case in point: while highly respected in fashion circles for her classic personal style, to many women she looked too hard, too thin, too groomed and too neat. Jennifer Saunders's character Edina Monsoon in the British sitcom *Absolutely Fabulous*, on the other hand, takes designer dressing too far: the curls, the frills, the colour and print combinations turn her into a fashion tsunami – the ultimate fashion victim.

Feminine dressing, perhaps more than any other style, buys into the myth of transformation. In the film *Pretty Woman* (1990) it was the feminine frocks that turned prostitute Vivian Ward, played by Julia Roberts, into a lady worth saving; a modern-day fairy tale in which Cinderella's dress is every bit as significant to the ultimate happy ending.

Valentino, whose designs featured in *Pretty Woman*, is a designer with an innate understanding of women and how to dress them. Not without reason has he been dubbed 'the master of the dress'. He is incredibly popular with European royalty, American socialites and big-name movie stars. Jackie Kennedy wore a white lace Valentino mini dress to marry Aristotle Onassis on a Greek island in 1968, and some of the world's most beautiful women across the decades have favoured his designs, including Elizabeth Taylor, Princess Diana, Sienna Miller, Uma Thurman and Nicole Kidman.

If you look at the must-have purchases of the last century, a large proportion are intrinsically feminine. There is a security in feminine dressing to which most women aspire, and although it may at times spill over into retrospective fantasy it is still a flattering look. Contemporary designers may regard femininity as an overrated cliché, but if sales are anything to go by, the consumer is still seduced by the concept. (After all, what looks good on a matchstick-thin model probably doesn't look so great on the vast majority of normal, womanly-shaped women.) The feminine dress does not dominate or titillate and is neither overstated nor overdone. And, more than any other kind, the feminine dress allows its wearer to shine through.

Above: First lady Jacqueline Kennedy at the Taj Mahal in 1962 during a trip to India and Pakistan. "Her every seam has been the subject of hypnotised attention from the streets of Delhi to the Khyber Pass", wrote Anne Chamberlain in *Life*. The location was later famously utilised by Princess Diana.

Left: Cecil Beaton's 1948 photograph of Charles James' gowns purposely evokes the portraits of an earlier, more gracious age. Described by Balenciaga as 'the world's best and only dressmaker', James was famous for his evening gowns, and for the creativity of their complex cut.

"*There has to be a first dress, like a first kiss; there has to be.*"

Justine Picardie, *My Mother's Wedding Dress: The Life and Afterlife of Clothes*

Right: Apollonia van Ravenstein models a Seventies gingham, floral and ric-rac combination, that perfectly illustrates the riotous mix of colour, print, pattern and detail in the girlish designs that typified the early seventies.

Above: This floral dress must represent the ultimate in Fifties femininity – but it's an appeal that never really goes away. To quote young US designer Erin Fetherston, interviewed for a piece on 'The New Feminine' in the British *Vogue* of May 2008: 'in the end, everyone just wants to look pretty'.

Right: White strapless ballgown by Christian Dior, 1952. White, the colour of innocence, has a particular place to play in feminine iconography and Dior was very aware of it: two years later, in 1954, he brought out his white 'Lily of the Valley' line.

Left: This Horst photograph of Jane Fonda looking quietly curvaceous in a plaid wool dress, c.1959, was taken before the launch of her acting career.

Right: Jean Paul Gaultier is a designer who refuses to conform and who is commonly associated with excess, yet many of his designs when removed from the catwalk are exquisitely beautiful and feminine, here fringe and floral appliqué from Jean Paul Gaultier's haute couture collection, 2007.

Right: Valentino, dubbed the 'Master of the Dress', surrounded by models in signature '*Valentino rosso*', in 1990. The designer is favoured by European royalty, American socialites and celebrities for his luxurious designs with their trademark flattering, refined yet body-conscious silhouettes.

Red Carpet

'The perfect dress is more loyal than the perfect man on the red carpet', says John Galliano, the man who has made so many. 'A great dress can make you look and feel amazing, bring you out of your shell and make you all the things you hope you are.' In recent years, the red carpet in general, and the Academy Awards ceremony in particular, has become the ultimate showcase for the Big Frock.

It hasn't always been that way. Janet Gaynor wore a knee-length knitted dress to collect her Best Actress award at the first ceremony in 1929; while in the early seventies, Jane Fonda – like Barbara Streisand just before her – opted for a trouser suit. But in between those patches of austerity this has usually been the night on which the film industry 'shows its face'. That's how it was put by *Dynasty* designer Nolan Miller, hired in the mid-Eighties as the Oscars' fashion consultant; and from Grace Kelly and Audrey Hepburn (left), waiting to present Academy Awards at the 1956 ceremony) to Penelope Cruz (above), in Atelier Versace, 2007 or Anne Hathaway in Marchesa (see over) at the 2008 ceremony, the stars have tended to agree.

Above: Keira Knightley in gold lame by Gucci at the premiere of *Pirates of the Caribbean: Dead Man's Chest*, 2006.

Above: Anne Hathaway, feminine in bold red Marchesa at the 80th Academy Awards, 2008.

Left: An earlier take on public glamour, Marlene Dietrich strikes a pose in a stiffened gold lamé dress, 1940.

chapter
EIGHT
Art

The line between fashion and other art forms has always been a fine one – if indeed it exists at all. This is a subject with mileage: while the pragmatic Chanel insisted couture was a profession, her rival Schiaparelli declared that 'Dress designing...is to me not a profession but an art.' Yves Saint Laurent once described his work as 'minor art', but later amended 'maybe it is not so minor after all'. Perhaps the uncertainty – and the urgency of the debate – reflects the fact that the making of clothes has only relatively recently stepped out of the shadows and taken its place as an act of creation. Historically dressmaking (like painting or sculpture many centuries before it) had been regarded as purely craft manufacture. The idea that a dressmaker might set up as an arbiter of taste was a new one when Rose Bertin, who made clothes for Marie Antoinette, was blamed for the extravagance of the French court. It was the second half of the nineteenth century before Charles Worth became effectively the first haute couturier, recognised for his imagination as much as his skill; and the twentieth before Poiret was hailed as 'the Sultan of fashion'.

Sometimes fashion clearly echoes other arts. Jeanne Lanvin owed a debt to Botticelli: the famous 'bleu Lanvin' can be seen in medieval art. Balenciaga's work has been discussed in terms of Velázquez (the 'Infanta' gowns he made before World War II), Zurbarán (his use of draping, and of muted monastic browns) and Goya (black lace, and the combination of pink and black).

Sixties' designers took direct inspiration from contemporary art, using bold colours and dynamic patterns, psychedelic florals and Bridget Riley-inspired prints. The dramatic black and white of much Op Art work, with its geometric designs and hallucinatory distortions, translated very well to textile design, and to dresses in the new stark shapes. Yves Saint Laurent famously reproduced art in his Mondrian dresses in 1965: 'the strict lines of the paintings go very well with the female body.' He followed them up with Pop Art dresses influenced by contemporary painters such as Tom Wesselmann and Andy Warhol, whose Flowers series was also adapted by American designer Halston.

Warhol himself reproduced his own paintings in the form of 'wearable art', and his work continued to inspire designers: in 1991 his images of Marilyn Monroe became a dress by Gianni Versace. In the seventies and eighties, the revolutionary aesthetic of Issey Miyake – whose work is often described as a kind of origami – and subsequent Japanese designers was informed by contemporary art. In 1996 Vivienne Westwood took inspiration from the colours, shapes and styles of Antoine Watteau for her 'Les Femmes' collection. And the first *Vogue* of 2008 declared that: 'Fashion and art collide in an explosion of painterly prints' – a statement borne out by almost every show of the season. Hand-painted frocks by Dolce & Gabbana were being photographed everywhere.

Sometimes the link between fashion and the other arts is nostalgic and reverential. In the late 1930s Norman Hartnell, acting on the suggestion of the new King George VI, used Winterhalter's portraits of the crinolined Empress Eugénie and the Empress Elisabeth of Austria as inspiration for the dresses he made for the then Queen Elizabeth, and the resultant 'picture' frocks were a staple of royal wardrobes for almost two decades. (Cecil Beaton, photographing the dresses of his old Harrovian friend the

> *"Fashion is at once both caterpillar and butterfly...There must be dresses that crawl and dresses that fly."*
> Coco Chanel

couturier Charles James, consciously echoed that same court of the Empress Eugénie.) But sometimes it is dynamic and revolutionary. Poiret's silhouette and colour palette in 1908 drew directly on the artistic events Paris had seen in the years immediately before: Isadora Duncan dancing in 1903; the first Fauves exhibition in 1905 and, in 1906, Diaghilev's first exhibition of Russian art.

In the Paris of the early twentieth century, couture was readily accepted as having intellectual implications. Jean Cocteau was proud to declare himself the muse of the designers; Colette and Andre Gide came to their shows. Several of the important early couturiers owed their inspiration to a fine art aesthetic rather than to an apprenticeship in dressmaking, notably Elsa Schiaparelli – 'the Italian artist who makes clothes', as Coco Chanel described her – whose collaboration with the Surrealists shows the ties between the visual forms most clearly.

Schiaparelli's skintight 'Skeleton' evening dress (1938) had a matt black surface decorated only by a padded trapunto exoskeleton, the bones 'worn' outside the clothes. Today, it evokes the black leather evening dress Thierry Mugler made in 1997, with its beetle-like articulated exoskeleton: at the time, it reflected the increasing application of the new ideas of psychology to clothing in the 1930s. Decorating a dress with notes of music, and basing one collection on the Commedia dell'Arte, Schiaparelli also worked directly with Jean Cocteau and, in jewellery, with the sculptor Giacometti. Her lovely butterfly-printed dress of the 1937 collection, with its theme of Metamorphosis, echoed a fascination with the creatures and with the idea of their change, shared by Max Ernst and Man Ray.

The famous 'Tear' dress (1938) used a fabric designed for Schiaparelli by Salvador Dali, with a *trompe l'oeil* motif of torn flesh, and a pink undergarment intended to represent the flesh beneath the skin. The theme had already appeared in Dali's painting *Three Young Surrealist Women Holding in Their Arms the Skins of an Orchestra*. Schiaparelli's shop in the Place Vendôme was, the artist wrote in his book *Eroticism in Clothing*, 'where the tongues of fire of the Holy Ghost of Dali were to descend'. Though Schiaparelli's designs were often playful – as in the dress adorned with a large lobster, and famously worn by the Duchess of Windsor – the Surrealists were also concerned to alert the world to the dark progress of Fascism: to the flesh ripped apart by militaristic repression or in war; to the beautiful things needlessly destroyed. A modern parallel might be the use of Chinese or Russian traditional costume by Yves Saint Laurent in the mid-seventies to lament the degree to which those countries, at that time, were rejecting their own pasts.

In discussing fashion in terms of art there is, too, the question of the artistry with which dresses are shown to the public. The illustrations that Poiret commissioned in 1908 to display his dresses were very modern, with their deliberate flatness and blocks of colour that echoed the

work of avant-garde artists like Gauguin and Matisse. They might even be said to have mirrored the stylised dramatisations of early Hollywood movies. Illustrations continued to challenge photographs as the best way to honour a couturier's artistic vision: as late as 1947 *Vogue* used an illustration for the cover of the issue that trumpeted Dior's New Look.

Even some of the earliest fashion photographs consciously position themselves in terms of the artistic world, and by the 1950s Irving Penn at *Vogue* and Richard Avedon at *Harper's Bazaar* helped set the look of the fashion decade, just as the more overtly sexual photographs of Helmut Newton and Bruce Weber did for a later generation. In the past few decades designers like Vivienne Westwood, Jean Paul Gaultier and John Galliano have found a secondary mode of expression in the catwalk shows they use to present their designs. Sometimes the display, the sheer dazzling extravaganza (and the consequent publicity for the global brand) seems almost more important than the display of the dresses – but then, the idea that the art of display could be at war with the needs of fashion is nothing new, as a 1938 memo from *Vogue* editor-in-chief Edna Woolman Chase to her photographers made clear: 'Concentrate completely on showing the dress, light it for this purpose and if that can't be done with art then art be damned. Show the dress. This is an order straight from the boss's mouth...'

The 1955 image of Dovima and the elephants, their curling trunks echoing the sinuous lines of her dress, is associated at least as much with Avedon's name as with that of Yves Saint Laurent (or indeed of the House of Dior, for which he was then working). In 1975 the *New York Times* observed that in Helmut Newton's photographs 'the interest in fashion is indistinguishable from an interest in murder, pornography and terror.'

One cannot leave this subject without discussing those dresses that seem to self-identify as art – making a statement that their creator has more on his or her mind than mere practicality. Experiments that appear to be designed only for the catwalk rather than the closet, working on a visual or theoretical level, with little concern for wearability. It is a matter of debate as to whether they should be considered in the same terms as more practical garments, or whether they should be regarded rather as gestures, equivalent to the dress made of rainbow-coloured condoms worn at a rally to raise consciousness of HIV.

Geoffrey Beene – whose own fiercely practical designs were created in the sixties and seventies, the era of the paper frock and the metal mini-dress – said that 'If clothes are not wearable they should have another name.' Except – and it is a big exception – that perhaps every adventure beyond accepted boundaries advances those

Page 165: Balenciaga was often inspired by Spanish painters like Velázquez or Goya; but these dresses of 1951, evoke, instead, the raffish Paris of Toulouse-Lautrec.

Left: Schiaparelli's 'Skeleton' evening dress of 1937 shows the influence of Surrealist ideas. The 'bones' which sit on the surface of skin-tight black crepe were created using the technique of trapunto quilting. The dress was to be worn with a long black veil, and a small gold snail shell.

boundaries to some degree. (And although the paper dresses of the late sixties had only a brief vogue, in their time they – like vinyl and PVC – were worn widely enough to spawn their own shop, the Waste Paper Boutique; several decades later Donna Karan used non-rip paper to make cocktail frocks.)

Extreme experimentation was nothing new, even before the sixties. Schiaparelli in the 1930s created a dress made with cellophane – something that still seemed daring when it was tried again in the 1960s. She made a necklace out of aspirin and buttons out of cinnamon: Moschino's 1988 dress made out of a petticoat and twenty bras could be no stranger. Designers have always been aware of the value of publicity, and of the dress that will draw the headlines. A collection needed not only its infinitely usable, go-anywhere 'Fords' (*Vogue* had dubbed the little black dress the Ford of fashion) but what Dior called its *'coups de Trafalgar'* – 'models that determine the fashion of today, and also that of tomorrow.' A look at the past should give pause to anyone today too eager to dismiss experimental designs as mere modern publicity stunts.

But all the same, the gulf between the high-octane experimental garments of some designers and high street fashion does seem wider than ever in the last few years. Alongside the romanticism of designers like Galliano runs an alternative strand: Gaultier's 'man frock'; Alexander McQueen's 2001 dress made out of razor shells. Hussein Chalayan presents ground-breaking designs in shows akin to performance art or installations; in one recent collection (courtesy of the robotics team who created the hippogriff in the film *Harry Potter and the Prisoner of*

Azkaban) the dresses themselves morphed – shorter, longer, tighter, broader – to give a ten-minute history of twentieth-century fashion.

A Chalayan dress may be made of ice or sugar and broken with a hammer on stage, of paper or of bubbles, or decorated with light-emitting diodes. Elements of Chalayan's revolutionary designs can be traced backwards. Forty years ago Mary Quant prophesied that some day we would blow clothes the way we blow glass, and Balenciaga made a wedding dress that would be inflated into a cone by the movement of the bride; more than eighty years ago Molyneux concealed electric light bulbs in the jewels of a harem dress. But they most definitely also look forward, and Chalayan's innovation excites even beyond the fashion industry. His bubble dress predates the latest creation from electronics giant Philips: a dress made of bubbles that purport to change colour with the wearer's mood.

Perhaps, as Karl Lagerfeld has said, the only thing that can be new about fashion today is the material. But that experimentation of one sort or another should exist is surely integral to the continued vitality of fashion. As Chanel put it many years ago: 'Fashion is at once both caterpillar and butterfly. Be a caterpillar by day and a butterfly by night...There must be dresses that crawl and dresses that fly.'

Right: Linda Evangelista in a Vivienne Westwood dress from 1995 inspired by the paintings of Antoine Watteau. It is made in green and purple shot silk faille and taffeta which Westwood advocates wearing crumpled, as if straight out of the suitcase.

Right: 'The series of exotic influences that fashion has soaked up throughout the 20th century have transformed the way we dress into a tangible map of the world', says Christian Lacroix. In the 2007–2008 collection, his own love of opulence and decoration finds echoes in the icons of old Russia.

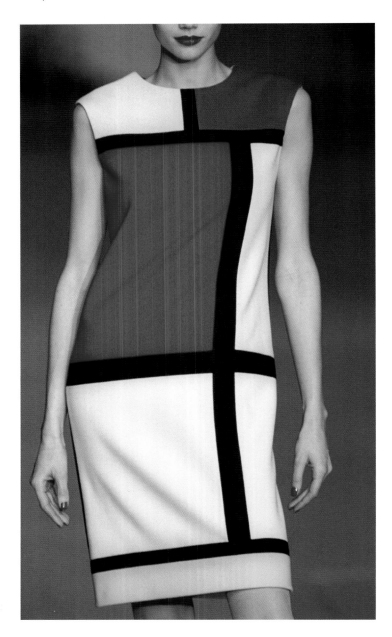

Above: Yves St Laurent's iconic dress, from the 1965–1966 collection, was inspired by the abstract paintings of the Dutch artist Mondrian. It was featured on the cover of French *Vogue* and widely copied.

Right: A major Op Art exhibition, 'The Responsive Eye' in the Museum of Modern Art, New York, caught the public attention and resulted in the style being utilised in television, advertising, interiors and fashion, as seen here from 1966.

Right: If Poiret abolished the corset at the start of the early twentieth century, Jean Paul Gaultier is credited with bringing it back into fashion some seventy years later. Gaultier cites his grandmother's corsetry as an ongoing source of inspiration and fascination, here from 1989.

Opposite: Paco Rabanne, who originally trained as an architect, is famed for his use of unconventional materials. Rabanne said that the 1991 collection, shown here, was inspired by the concept of recycling, but, in contrast to the eco-friendly ethos that his words suggest, this dress speaks of armour and aggression.

Above: Automotive corset dress, 1989, by Thierry Mugler, who takes inspiration from Hollywood glamour, science fiction, and sexual fetishism, as well as fifties automobile design. His creations are always dramatic and extravagant, and often rigid in construction to distort and exaggerate the silhouette.

Following page, left: 'In the world today haute couture is one of the last repositories of the marvellous', said Christian Dior, 'and the couturiers the last possessors of the wand of Cinderella's Fairy Godmother.' Here Gaultier shows a living work of art using fresh foliage from his haute couture collection, 2002.

Following page, right: For their 2008 collection, Dolce & Gabbana hired young artists to hand-paint their own designs – from abstracts to florals – onto silk, as though it were canvas. The results have been made up into dresses in 'limited edition' runs. This is literally art you can wear.

*"Trends are boring
and transient. I am interested
in clothes, not fashion."*
Hussein Chalayan

Previous page: Hussein Chalayan's thoughtful designs are a conceptual mix of fashion and art, seen here his 'Motorized airplane dress 100% fibre glass' 1999–2000. Chalayan says: 'Trends are boring and transient. I am interested in clothes, not fashion.'

Left: Issey Miyake's sculptural work creates designs that are an art in themselves, but which are given a new dimension of life and movement when worn, here from 1997–1998.

Timeline

1908–'17

1918–'27

Poiret's abolition of the corset signals the birth of modern fashion: in 1908 the publication of *Les Robes de Paul Poiret* spreads his message further afield. In 1911 he introduces the massively influential hobble skirt; followed by the lampshade tunic and the Minaret dress. But the outbreak of World War I in 1914 brings in change in mood to fashion: 1915 sees the start of a trend for fuller, A-line skirts ending just above the ankle, more practical for women forced into the wartime workplace. The designers who, after 1918, attempted to recreate pre-war styles would be doomed to fail.

In 1920 the hemline rises to an unprecedented 3 inches above the ankle and (with one brief return to ground level) continues to rise. In 1925 the waistline drops below the hips: in 1927 it disappears altogether, and skirts reach just below the knee. Coco Chanel first establishes herself as a couturier in 1919 and becomes ever more prominent through the decade. In 1925 she presents a high-necked, long-sleeved black frock which *Vogue* hails as the new wardrobe staple, the Little Black Dress. Paris is now dominated by female couturiers: Chanel, Jeanne Lanvin, Madeleine Vionnet, Alix Grès, the Callot Soeurs. Jeanne Paquin withdraws from business, but Elsa Schiaparelli creates her first design.

1928–'37

1938–'47

In the US, Hattie Carnegie launches her first ready-to-wear collection in 1928; couture suffers in the wake of the Wall Street Crash of 1929 and style takes on a more conservative tone. Hemlines drop back down to mid-calf for day wear, ground length for evening, and the waist resumes its proper place. Madeleine Vionnet's exploration of the bias cut becomes increasingly influential, as does Hollywood style, especially in its more elaborate and overtly seductive aspects. In 1932 Macy's sells a reputed half million copies of the dress Joan Crawford wears in *Letty Lynton*. In 1937 the dress Mainbocher designs for the wedding of Wallis Simpson and the Duke of Windsor is copied everywhere; while the same year Schiaparelli, in collaboration with the Surrealists, presents her 'Metamorphosis' collection and introduces the colour 'shocking' pink.

In 1939 the Paris collections feature fitted waists and crinoline skirts, just as *Gone With the Wind* comes out on screen. But the outbreak of World War II calls a halt to the movement, bringing in more masculine and practical designs. 1941 in Britain sees the first collection of fabric-saving 'Utility' clothes. In America, meanwhile, in 1942 Claire McCardell makes the enduringly relevant, pinafore-style 'Popover' dress; with Paris under German occupation, America is forced to continue developing its own style. But after liberation Paris moves to reassert its pre-eminence: in 1947 Christian Dior presents his 'Corolle' collection, soon known as the 'New Look'.

1948–'57

1958–'67

The great couturiers dominate the decade, ringing the changes on the silhouette with almost every collection. In 1951 Balenciaga shows a tent dress (and Italian couture enters the market place); in 1953 Dior introduces the form-fitting 'Tulipe' line; in 1954 Balenciaga presents the narrow I-shaped line and Dior the H-line, followed by the A-line and the Y-line. Fath and Balmain in Europe, Charles James in the States, are creating beautiful cocktail and evening frocks. But Balenciaga and his protégé Givenchy have also been developing versions of the less restrictive chemise and sack dresses, showing the way ahead even before the sudden death of Christian Dior in 1957 signals the end of an era. Several houses are starting to create designs specifically for the youth market: in 1955, in London, Mary Quant opens her first boutique.

After the acclaimed Trapeze line in 1958 youth fashion comes to the fore; St Laurent produces 'Beat' collection for Dior in 1960. Yuri Gagarin orbits the earth in 1961; in 1964 Courrèges shows 'Space Age' collection. Skirt lengths rise ever upwards and in 1965 Mary Quant's mini-dresses stop traffic on Times Square. In 1967 St Laurent shows the ethnic inspired 'Africa' collection. New labels launched include Bill Blass (1959); both St Laurent and Valentino (1962); and Jean Muir (1966). Others make their mark in radical new shops: Barbara Hulanicki at Biba (1964), Betsey Johnson at Paraphernalia (1965) and Laura Ashley (1967). Style icons range from Jackie Kennedy to Twiggy and influential films include *Breakfast at Tiffany's* (1961) and *Bonnie and Clyde* (1967).

1968–'77

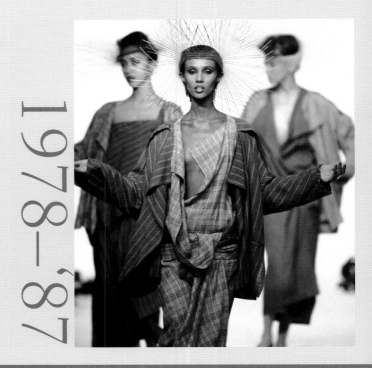

1978–'87

In 1969 Woodstock happens and the hippy revolution, ethnic and vintage anti-fashion cultures develop. Anything goes from the shortest of skirts to the floor skimming maxi. Thirties influences take a hold, led by Biba, as does the glam rock influence of pop. Halston introduces simple sexy jersey dresses for the disco generation, Diane Von Furstenberg launches the wrap dress and the punk revolution startles London. Calvin Klein (1968), Ralph Lauren (1972), and Giorgio Armani (1975) launch womenswear lines and Issey Miyake shows his first Paris collection in 1973. New shops opening include Norma Kamali (1968), Kenzo's Jungle Jap (1970), Vivienne Westwood and Malcolm McLaren's Let it Rock (1971) changed to Sex (1974) and Seditionaries (1976). Biba closes down in 1975. Film influences include *Barbarella* (1968), *The Great Gatsby* (1974), *Annie Hall* and Derek Jarman's *Jubilee* (both 1977).

Claude Montana and Thierry Mugler push Amazonian silhouettes with tight waists and mighty shoulders; a look popularised by TV soaps *Dallas* (1978) and *Dynasty* (1981). Lady Diana marries Prince Charles in a fairytale frock (1981). Yohji Yamamoto and Comme des Garçons (debut Paris shows both 1981) offer 'post-nuclear' chic. Gaultier launches own label in 1978, first shows conical bra dress in 1983. Azzedine Alaïa produces own line in 1980, perfect for the toned bodies of the new fitness fanatics and Vivienne Westwood shows 'Pirates', her first collection in 1981. Karl Lagerfeld label established and John Galliano's graduation collection creates frenzy (both 1984). Other new labels include Donna Karan and Dolce & Gabbana (both 1985), Helmut Lang (1986) and Marc Jacobs (1987). Christian Lacroix opens couture house (1987).

1988–'97

1998–2007

The new breed of toned celebrity supermodel shows off slick, body conscious and sexually provocative dresses. Evening dresses are back, as exemplified by the black lace Christina Stambolian 'take that' dress that Princess Diana dons in June 1994. Tom Ford is made Design Director of Gucci (1992), Westwood turns out statement evening wear with her Watteau inspired collection (1994), John Galliano shows the slip dress in his first collection for Dior and Diane Von Furstenberg launches the second generation wrap dress (both 1997). The film *Pretty Woman* sells the allure of the dress and Liz Hurley steals the limelight in Versace at the premiere of *Four Weddings and a Funeral* (1994).

The dress is back in the news: fifties and seventies influences dominate, and jersey wrap dresses are wardrobe staples. Roland Mouret reintroduces the allure of the strict, tailored dress for day. Evening glamour moves up a notch and big dresses make a comeback. Second hand becomes desirable 'vintage'; Julia Roberts wears vintage Valentino to collect her Oscar for *Erin Brokovitch*. Fashion looks backwards with the 60th anniversary of the launch of Dior, Valentino's retrospective, the 'Haute Couture' exhibition at the Victoria & Albert museum and Lacroix's 'Histories of Fashion' at the *Musée des Arts Décoratifs*. Hussein Chalayan is named British Designer of the Year (1999 and 2000) and Alexander McQueen named International Designer of the Year (2003). *Sex and the City* hits the TV screens (1998) and celebrates the joy of dressing up.

Index

Absolutely Fabulous 148
Adrian 54, 68, 79, 98, 99
Aguilera, Christina 105, 129
Alaïa, Azzedine 41, 47, 77, 124
Alexander, Hilary 129
Altman, Robert 136
Amies, Hardy 144
Angel 98
Armani, Giorgio 66, 82, 83
Ashley, Laura 59, 62, 101–2, 144
Associated Press 58
Avedon, Richard 169

Bacall, Lauren 146
Baker, Carroll 23
Bakst, Léon 14
Balenciaga, Cristobal 19, 23, 27, 54, 57, 66, 99, 123,
        146, 151, 166, 169, 170
Ballets Russes 14, 98
Balmain 144
Banton, Travis 57
Barbarella 36
Barbier, Georges 146
Bardot, Brigitte 58, 59
Berenson, Marisa 62
Bazaar 58
Beatles 62, 105
Beaton, Cecil 23, 51, 151, 166–7
Beauvoir, Simone de 8
Beckham, Victoria 66, 129
Beene, Geoffrey 77, 80, 169
Benaim, Laurence 77, 86
Berenson, Marisa 145
Bergdorf Goodman 37
Bergen, Candice 62
Berketex 56
Bertin, Rose 166
Biba 59, 102, 106, 145
Birell, Tala 73
Birkin, Jane 130

Birtwell, Celia 36, 41, 66
Björk 148
Blass, Bill 46, 83
Bohan, Marc 58
Bonnie and Clyde 102
Botticelli, Sandro 166
Boyfriend 102
Breakfast at Tiffany's 8, 73, 79
Brook, Kelly 134
Bündchen, Gisele 134
Burchill, Julie 105, 115

Callot Soeurs 91
Campbell, Naomi 43, 134
Capote, Truman 73
Cardin, Pierre 36, 51, 99, 105
Carnegie, Hattie 23, 54
Cassini, Oleg 79, 91
Chalayan, Hussein 170, 182, 185
Chamberlain, Anne 149
Chanel, Coco 8, 14, 17, 20–3, 36, 54, 58, 62, 65, 66,
        71, 93, 98, 102, 166, 167, 170
Charles, Prince of Wales 115, 146
Charrier, Jacques 58
Chase, Edna Woolman 169
Chloé 102
Christie, Julie 59
Clark, Ossie 36, 41, 106
Cocteau, Jean 167
Colette 167
Comme des Garçons 37
Commedia Dell'Arte 167
Constant Gardener 62
Cooper, Lady Diana 14
Courrèges, André 34, 36, 39, 58, 99
Crawford, Cindy 46
Crawford, Joan 54, 68, 98
Cruz, Penelope 161
Cunningham, Bill 144

Daily Mirror 58
Dali, Savador 120, 167
Dallas 41, 45, 124
Dawney, Jean 11
De Niro, Robert 65
Demeulemeester, Ann 41, 42
Dennis, Felix 130
Derry & Toms 59
Diaghilev, Sergei 14, 167
Diana, Princess of Wales 8, 73, 41, 66, 105, 115, 146, 148, 149
Dietrich, Marlene 77, 98, 163
DiMaggio, Joe 139
Dior, Christian 5, 8, 14, 23, 25, 28, 66, 34, 57, 120, 144, 155, 170, 179
    House of Dior 11, 27, 42, 47, 58, 105, 106, 145, 169
    New Look 11, 19–20, 27, 57, 98, 99, 123, 146, 169
Dolce and Gabbana 8, 31, 43, 129, 134, 166, 179
Dolce, Domenico 46
Dors, Diana 31
Dovima 169
Duncan, Isadora 77, 167
Dynasty 41, 45, 124, 161

e e cummings 91
Elisabeth, Empress of Austria 166
Elizabeth II 80, 98, 146
Elizabeth, Queen Mother 146, 166
Elle 20
Emanuel, Elizabeth and David 105, 146
Erin Brockovich 148
Ernst, Max 167
Erté 51
Eugénie, Empress 166, 167
Evangelista, Linda 5, 170

Fashion Today 76
Fath, Jacques 5, 144
Father of the Bride 115
Fauves 14, 167
Fetherston, Erin 154
Fonda, Jane 156, 161
Fonteray, Jacques 36
Ford, Betty 62
Ford, Tom 80, 129
Fortuny, Mariano 76, 98
Four Weddings and a Funeral 122, 124
Fratini, Gina 62
French, Marilyn *The Women's Room* 36

Gabbana, Stefano 46
Gagarin, Yuri 36
Galliano, John 11, 42, 47, 48, 105, 106, 115, 145, 161, 169, 170
Gallico, Paul *Flowers for Mrs Harris* 8, 120

Garbo, Greta 77
Garland, Ailsa *Lion's Share* 80
Gauguin, Paul 167
Gaultier, Jean Paul 41, 83, 105, 120, 129, 156, 169, 170, 176, 179
Gaynor, Janet 161
Gazette du Bon Ton 14, 146
George VI 166
Giacometti, Alberto 167
Gibb, Bill 101, 102
Gide, Andre 167
Gigli, Romeo 146
Ginger Group 58
Giroud, Françoise 20
Givenchy, Hubert de 8, 23, 54, 79
Glyn, Elinor 98
Gone With the Wind 99
Goya, Francisco 166, 169
Grant, Hugh 122
Grease 54
Great Gatsby 102
Green, Felicity 58
Greene, Alexander Plunket 123
Grès, Madame 17, 76, 86, 124
Grisewood, Freddie 80
Gucci 41, 62, 80, 129, 163

Hall, Jerry 8, 136
Halliwell, Geri 134
Halston 62, 80, 83, 86, 89, 166
Hamnett, Katharine 120
Harper's Bazaar 20, 54, 57, 169
Harry Potter and the Prisoner of Azkaban 170
Hartnell, Norman 56, 80, 98, 166
Harvey, Anna 105
Hathaway, Anne 161, 163
Head, Edith 8, 79
Heals 59
Hepburn, Audrey 8, 73, 79, 161
Hepburn, Katherine 77
Hilton, Nicky 115
Hilton, Paris 134
Hollywood 17, 19, 54–7, 77–9, 98–9
Horst 23, 156
Hulanicki, Barbara 34, 58–9, 106
Hulanicki, Fitz 59
Hurley, Elizabeth 66, 120, 122, 124

Iribe, Paul *Les Robes de Paul Poiret* 98

J. C. Penney 58
Jagger, Bianca 80
Jagger, Jade 62
James, Charles 51, 144, 151, 167
Janowitz, Tama 123, 134

Jarman, Derek 124
Johansson, Scarlett 66, 93
Johnson, Beverley 86
Jordan 124
Jubilee 124

Kane, Christopher 136
Kaner, Joan 37
Karan, Donna 83, 170
Kawakubo, Rei 37, 41, 76
Kee, Jenny 37
Keenan, Bridget 101
Kelly, Grace 115, 146, 161
Kennedy, Jackie 58, 61, 79, 80, 91, 148, 149
Kennedy, John Fitzgerald 79, 91, 139
Kidman, Nicole 83, 148
Klein's Cash and Carry 54
Klein, Calvin 46, 80–3
Knightley, Keira 163

Lacroix, Christian 8, 172
    On Fashion 105
Ladies Home Journal 58
Lagerfeld, Karl 66, 102, 170
Lang, Helmut 83
Lanvin, Jeanne 17, 166
Lauren, Ralph 102
Laver, James 120
Lelong, Lucien 17, 19, 31, 120
Lepape, Georges 14
Letty Lynton 54, 68
Levy, Ariel 129
Liberty 59
Life 25, 54, 58, 61, 149
Lombard, Carole 57
Los Angeles Times 102
Lucile (Lady Duff Gordon) 98

Macdonald, Julien 129, 134
Macy's 54
Madonna 62, 105, 129
Mailer, Norman 139
Mainbocher 19, 54
Man Ray 167
Marchesa 161, 163
Margaret, Princess 146
Margiela, Martin 41
Marie Antoinette 166
Marie Antoinette 98
Martin, Richard 124
Mary of Scotland 57
Matisse, Henri 167
McCardell, Claire 8, 19, 20, 57–8, 66, 68, 76, 79, 89
McCartney, Stella 93
McDowell, Colin 37, 76, 105, 129

McLaren, Malcolm 124
McQueen, Alexander 110, 170
Melly, George 99
Messel, Oliver 98
Miller, Lee 31
Miller, Nolan 161
Miller, Sienna 148
Minogue, Kylie 62, 129, 134
Missoni, Rosita 37, 66, 129, 146
Miyake, Issey 37, 51, 76, 166, 185
Molyneux 19, 170
Mondrian, Piet 166, 174
Monroe, Marilyn 139, 146, 166
Montana, Claude 41, 124
Morehouse, Marion 71, 91
Moschino 170
Moss, Kate 46
Motion Picture Studio Insider 54
Mountbatten, Edwina 115
Mouret, Roland 8, 62, 66
Mugler, Thierry 41, 45, 124, 136, 167, 178
Muir, Jean 80

New Look 11, 19–20, 27, 57, 98, 99, 123, 146, 169
New York Times 169
Newsweek 65
Newton, Helmut 169
Niagara 139
Norell, Norman 79–80
Nova 101

Oldfield, Bruce 8
Oliver, Andre 105
Onassis, Aristotle 148
Op Art 66, 166, 174
Orry-Kelly 139
Other Boleyn Girl 93
Oz 130
Ozbek, Rifat 101

Paley, Babe 80
Paquin, Jeanne 14, 76, 146
Parker, Sarah Jessica 43
Parkinson, Norman 8
Patou, Jean 17
Penn, Irving 169
Perls, Frank 77
Philadelphia Story 77
Philips 170
Picardie, Justine *My Mother's Wedding Dress: the Life and Afterlife of Clothes* 144, 152
Pidgeon, Walter 73
Pirates of the Caribbean: Dead Man's Chest 163
Plunkett, Walter 57
Poiret, Paul 14, 51, 76, 98, 120, 166, 167–9, 176

Pop Art 166
Porter, Thea 62
Prêt à Porter 136
Pretty Woman 148
Pucci, Emilio 36, 66, 145–6
Pulitzer, Lilly 58, 61

Quant, Mary 17, 23, 34, 58, 123, 170

Rabanne, Paco 31, 36, 176
Rainier III of Monaco 115
Reagan, Nancy 41
Renta, Oscar de la 80
Rhianna 129
Rhodes, Zandra 36–7, 62, 101, 124
Rhumba 57
Rhys, Jean 8
Rigg, Frank 91
Riley, Bridget 166
Roberts, Julia 148
Rochas, Marcel 19, 54
Rolling Stone 123
Romeo and Juliet 98
Romero, Cesar 73
Rose, Helen 115
Russell, Ken 102

Saab, Elie 93
Saint Laurent, Yves 23, 27, 34, 98, 101, 105, 112,
    120, 123, 129, 166, 167, 169, 174
Sander, Jil 83
Saunders, Jennifer 148
Schiaparelli, Elsa 17, 54, 76, 77, 79, 98, 120, 166,
    167, 169, 170
Schiffer, Claudia 93
Sear 57
Seven Year Itch 139
SEX 124
Sex and the City 42–3
She's Dangerous 73
Shearer, Norma 98
Sheppard, Cybill 65
Shrimpton, Jean 34
Simpson, Wallis 54, 148, 167
Snow, Carmel 20, 28
Some Like it Hot 139
Spears, Britney 129
Stambolian, Christina 73, 146
Stefani, Gwen 115
Steinem, Goria 62
Stevenson, Adlai 139, 140
Storey, Helen 62, 144
Streisand, Barbara 161
Surrealism 167

Takada, Kenzo 37, 101
Taxi Driver 65
Taylor, Elizabeth 62, 105, 115, 146, 148
Thatcher, Margaret 80
Thurman, Uma 148
Time 27
Toulouse-Lautrec, Henri 169
Tuffin, Sally 34
Turner, Lana 139
Twiggy 8, 59, 102, 123

Ungaro, Emanuel 99

Valentino 5, 148, 158
Valetta, Amber 91
Van Ravenstein, Apollonia 153
Velásquez, Diego 99, 166, 169
Versace, Donatella 129
Versace, Gianni 8, 41, 62, 76, 83, 91, 120, 122, 124,
    129, 132, 136, 161, 166
Versailles 27, 47
Vionnet, Madeleine 14, 17, 23, 42, 76, 77, 84, 86,
    122, 124
Vogue 17, 19, 20, 34, 36, 54, 57, 66, 76, 80, 86, 98, 99,
    102, 105, 144, 154, 166, 169, 170, 174
Von Furstenberg, Diane 62, 65, 66, 145
Vreeland, Diana 79, 80, 126

Warhol, Andy 80, 166
Waste Paper Boutique 170
Watanabe, Junya 76
Watteau, Antoine 99, 166, 170
Weber, Bruce 169
Weisz, Rachel 62, 66
Wesselmann, Tom 166
Westwood, Vivienne 37, 41, 45, 99, 102, 110, 124, 129,
    166, 169, 170
Wilder, Billy 79
Williams, Tennessee 23
Wilson, Elizabeth *Adorned in Dreams* 102
Windsor, Duchess of 54, 148, 167
Winterhalter, Franz 166
Wolfe, Tom 36
Woman and Beauty 66
Women's Wear Daily 79, 99, 101, 110, 122
Worth, Charles 166

Yamamoto, Yohji 37
Young, Richard 122

Zurbáran, Francisco 166

Bibliography

Ashelford, Jane, *The Art of Dress: Clothes and Society 1500 – 1914* The National Trust 1996

Bailey, Margaret J., *Those Glorious Glamour Years: Classic Hollywood Costume Design in the 1930s* Columbus 1982

Barwick, Sandra, *A Century of Style* George Allen & Unwin 1984

Benaim, Lawrence, *Gres* Assouline 1999

Bowles, Hamish, *Jacqueline Kennedy: The White House Years*, Little Brown and Company, 2001

Breward, Christopher, *The Culture of Fashion*, Manchester University Press, 1995

Breward, Christopher, *Fashion*, Oxford University Press 2003

Buxbaum, Gerda (ed), *Icons of Fashion*, Prestel 1999

Chase, Edna Woolman and Ilka, *Always in Vogue*, Gollancz 1964

Colbin, Pamela, *Fashion Designers*, Watson-Gupthill Publications

Cosgrave, Bronwyn, *Made for Each Other: Fashion and the Academy Awards*, Bloomsbury 2007

Cunnington, C. W., *English Women's Clothing in the Present Century*, Faber & Faber 1952

De La Haye, Amy, *The Cutting Edge, 50 Years of British Fashion*, V&A Publications, 1996

Dior, Christian, *Dior by Dior*, Harmondsworth 1958

Edelman, Amy Holman, *The Little Black Dress*, Simon & Schuster, 1997

Ewing, Elizabeth, *History of 20th Century Fashion*, Batsford, 2005

The Fashion Book, Phaidon, 1998

Golbin, Pamela, *Fashion Designers*, Watson-Guptill Publications, 2001

Jouve, Marie-Andrée and Jacqueline Demornex, *Balenciaga*, Thames & Hudson 1989

Kamitsis, Lydia, *Vionnet*, Thames & Hudson 1996

Koda, Harold, *Extreme Beauty: The Body Transformed*, The Metropolitan Museum of Art 2001

Lacroix, Christian, *On Fashion*, Thames & Hudson 2007

Laver, James, *Costume and Fashion, A Concise History*, Thames & Hudson, 1982

Laver, James, *Modesty in Dress*, Heinemann 1969

Martin, Richard, *Charles James*, Assouline, 1997

McDowell, Colin, *Diana Style*, Aurum Press Ltd, 2007

McDowell, Colin, *Dressed to Kill: Sex, Power and Clothes*, Random Century Group Ltd, 1992

McDowell, Colin, *Fashion Today*, Phaidon Press, 2000

McDowell, Colin, *Forties Fashion and the New Look*, Bloomsbury 1997

McDowell, Colin, *The Literary Companion to Fashion*, Sinclair-Stevenson, 1995

Mackrell, Alison, *An Illustrated History of Fashion*, Batsford 1997

McDowell, Colin, *Ralph Lauren*, Cassell Illustrated, 1988

Mendes, Valerie and De La Haye, Amy, *20th Century Fashion*, Thames & Hudson, 1999

Modlinger, Jackie, *Diana Woman of Style*, Colour Library Direct, 1998

Mulvagh, Jane, *Vogue History of 20th Century Fashion*, Bloomsbury, 1988

Robinson, Julian, *The Golden Age of Style*, Orbis, 1976

Picardie, Justine, *My Mother's Wedding Dress: The Afterlife of Clothes*, Picador, 2005

Pochna, Marie-France, *Dior*, Thames & Hudson 1996Quant, Mary, *Quant by Quant*, Cassell, 1966

Turner, Lowri K, *Gianni Versace*, Essential, 1997

Scheips, Charlie, *American Fashion*, Assouline, 2007

Steele, Valerie, *Fifty Years of Fashion*, Yale University Press, 1997

Vintage Fashion, Carlton, 2006

Wilcox, Claire (ed.), *The Golden Age of Couture: Paris and London 1947 - 1957*, V&A Publications, 2007

Wood, Ghislaine, *The Surreal Body: Fetish and Fashion*, V&A Publications, 2007

Zilkha, Bettina, *Ultimate Style*, Assouline, 2004

Wilson, Elizabeth, *Adorned in Dreams: Fashion and Modernity*, Virago 1985

Acknowledgements

The publishers would like to thank the following individuals and organisations for supplying images for this book.

Cover images: Front: V&A Images/John French;
Back: Corbis/Condé Nast Archive/Horst P. Horst.
Endpapers: Corbis/Kim Kyung Hoon/Reuters.

Image Courtesy of the Advertising Archives 63; **akg-images** /© 2008 ADAGP Paris, DACS 13; **Camera Press London** /Frederic Bukajlo/Gamma 10, /Pascal Chevallier/Top 158-159, /Francoise Huguier/RAPHO 97, /Keystone – France 51 bottom, /Daniel Simon/Gamma 51 top right, 184-185, 190 right; **Catwalking.com** 31 top right, 82, 94, 112, 176, 183, 191 right; **Corbis** /Mario Anzuoni/Reuters 161, /Michel Arnaud 45, 47, 93, 95 left, 191 left, /Peter Andrews 163 left, /Bettmann 104, 114, 115 bottom left, 141, /Stephane Cardinale/People Avenue 108-109, 110, 157, /Cat's Collection 139 bottom, /Jean Jacques Ceccarini/epa 127, /Julio Donoso 4, 177, 178-179, /Peter Foley/epa 81, /Rune Hellestead 134, /Hulton-Deutsch Collection 55, 115 top right, /Douglas Kirkland 71, /Joel Landau 89, /Richard Melloul 137, /Genevieve Naylor 69, 88, /Thierry Orban 125, 132, 136, 174, 180, /Jean Paul Pelissier 173, /Bruno Pellerin/epa 49, /Quadrillion/David Levinson 116-117, /Vittoriano Rastelli 46 right, /Reuters 111, 135, /John Springer Collection 72, 162, /Stapleton Collection 147, /Sunset Boulevard/Sygma 139 top, /SYGMA 73 right, /Frank Trapper 163 right, /Pierre Vauthey/SYGMA 42-43, /Daniel Dal Zennaro/epa 181; **Corbis/Condé Nast Archive** /Cecil Beaton 50, 150-151, /Henry Clarke 2, 29, 78, 143, 189 left, /Horst P. Horst 16, 22, 73 top left, 75, 113, 133, 156, /George Hoyningen-Huene 30, /Frances McLauglin-Gill 26, 155, /Kourken Pakchanian 190 left, /Gosta Peterson 67, /Roger Prigent 154, /John Rawlings 6-7, 18, 21, 53, /Richard Rutledge 27, /Edward Steichen 15, 70, 85, 92, 187 right, 188 left; **Norman Eales** 100; **Philippe Garner Archive** 31 bottom, 131, 146, 187 left; **Getty Images** /Slim Aarons/Hulton Archive 60-61, /John T. Barr 46 left, /Jayne Fincher 73 bottom left, /Nick Giordano/Hulton Archive 175, /Dave Hogan 95 right, /M J Kim 62, /Popperfoto 56, 188 right, /Time & Life Pictures 9, 24-25, 38-39, 87, 119, 160, 165, /Justin de Villeneuve/Hulton Archive 103; **John F. Kennedy Presidential Library and Museum, Boston** /Robert Knudsen 90, /Cecil Stoughton 149; **Peter Knapp** 44; **The Kobal Collection** 64; **Courtesy of Missoni** /Mert Alas & Marcus Piggot 128; **Norman Parkinson Archive** 40, 153; **Photofest** 121; **Rex Features** /Everett Collection 68, 138, /Sharok Hatami 33, 189 right, /Tim Rooke 122, /Steve Wood 171, /Zandarin and Allen 115 top left; **TopFoto** /Topham Picturepoint 31 top left, 107, /Roger Viollet 51 top left, 86; **V&A Images** 168, /John French 35.

We apologise in advance for any unintentional omission or neglect and will be pleased to insert the appropriate acknowledgement for any companies or individuals in any subsequent edition of this work.

First published in the United Kingdom in 2008 by
PAVILION BOOKS
10 Southcombe Street, London, W14 0RA

An imprint of Anova Books Company Ltd

Design and layout © Pavilion, 2008
Text © Jane Eastoe and Sarah Gristwood, 2008
Photography © see acknowledgements on page 197

Senior editor: Emily Preece-Morrison
Designer: Georgina Hewitt
Picture researcher: Emma O'Neill
Copy editor: Maggie Ramsay
Indexer: Helen Snaith
Production: Rebekah Cheyne

ISBN 978-1-862057-98-2

A CIP catalogue record for this book is available
from the British Library.

10 9 8 7 6 5 4 3 2 1

Reproduction by Dot Gradations Ltd, UK
Printed and bound by Craftprint, Singapore

www.anovabooks.com